BASICS

FASHION DES

Jennifer Prendergast

SEWING TECHNIQUES

An introduction to construction skills within the design process

UNIVERSITY OF
GLOUCESTERSHIRE

at Cheltenham and Gloucester

B L O O M S B U R Y

0.1
Pierre Cardin, 1968
Three-dimensional dress
formed by heating the fabric
to form the shapes within
the bodice and hem.

Fairchild Books
An imprint of Bloomsbury Publishing Plc

50 Bedford Square   1385 Broadway
London   New York
WC1B 3DP   NY 10018
UK   USA

www.bloomsbury.com

Bloomsbury is a registered trademark of
Bloomsbury Publishing Plc

First published 2014

© Bloomsbury Publishing, 2014

**British Library
Cataloguing-in-Publication Data**

A catalogue record for this book is available from
the British Library.

ISBN:
PB: 978-2-940411-91-7
ePDF: 978-2-940447-71-8

**Library of Congress
Cataloging-in-Publication Data**

Prendergast, Jennifer.
Sewing techniques / Jennifer Prendergast.
pages cm

Includes bibliographical references and index.

ISBN 978-2-940411-91-7 (pbk.)
ISBN 978-2-940447-71-8 (epdf)
1. Machine sewing. I. Title.
TT713.P386 2014
646.2'044—dc23

2013042962

Designed by John F McGill, London

Cover image used with courtesy of Laurence Laborie

Printed and bound in China

Contents

Introduction
006

Increasingly, many designers are including sewing techniques throughout the design process, from research to final conception, as an art form and creative skill that informs their designs. These techniques range from traditional to innovative technological processes.

Sewing techniques covered in this book range from the exquisite hand-executed skills of haute couture to those used in the creation of ethically reconstructed garments. Each stage of the book will provide you with an overview of some of the processes involved. You will be taken through some of the basic sewing techniques but the emphasis throughout the book will be on self-development and experimentation.

The aim of the book is to help you to develop a sample portfolio that can be used to enhance your research, and to assist in the design development process and your garment development. Understanding some of the different sewing techniques is important but as you grow more confident in your skills, you will start to develop a unique signature to your work.

0.3
Beate Godager Interior/ Exterior 2010–05
White organza dress with pleated sleeves and discreet invisible zips inserted into front armhole.

Sewing Techniques: An introduction to construction skills within the design process will give you an overview of basic seam sample development, dart manipulation and professional finishes as well as technological advances in construction techniques. The interviews and case studies will reveal how designers use sewing techniques within their design work, each one following an individual process. You will also learn how to identify some of the equipment and machinery used and be given an insight into how some of the mechanisms work, which is vital to trouble-free sewing.

Sewing Techniques: An introduction to construction skills within the design process provides just one of several possible approaches to the construction of garments; however, starting with the basics will lead to more exciting and distinctive outcomes.

0.2
Elie Saab, Haute Couture, S/S 2013
Signature intricate lace embellishments. Dress with lace bodice and shoulder details, elegant coat with an appliquéd neckline and a delicate tulle embroidered dress with three-quarter length sleeves.

Planning

Planning the project

From conception to catwalk, the fashion industry thrives on the energy and buzz of each collection; therefore, adhering to deadlines is important. For all fashion designers, planning and preparation are essential. Prior planning allows the designer to concentrate on the creative process without any distractions. Within the fashion supply chain there are different approaches to planning but in most companies a computerized critical path is used. However, you may wish to use a more simple form, whereby the critical dates are written in a diary and checked regularly to ensure that you are working to schedule.

Make a list of essential items that you will need for the sewing project. This could include the following, depending on your own personal requirements:

× Needles: machine and hand stitching
× Spare spool and bobbin case
× Threads
× Notions/trims
× Tape measure
× Pins
× Dress form/mannequin
× Technical/working drawings
× Camera/notepad: for recording and reflection of the processes
× Any visual inspiration, such as sketches or photographs.

1.2
Industrial sewing needle
Close-up of an industrial sewing needle on a lockstitch machine. Lockstitch machines are the most popular industrial machine in any studio or factory. However, there are specialist machines, such as the one shown here, which are used to produce leather goods. This machine requires a leather needle, which is tougher than a normal needle and uses thicker, more durable thread for stitching leather.

1.2

'Before beginning, plan carefully.'

Marcus Tullius Cicero
(106-43 BC) Roman orator, writer, and politician.

1.3

Modelling on the stand
The designer models calico on the stand as part of the design process. This type of fabric manipulation is a form of silhouette development and can be part of the design research process. This hands-on approach allows the designer to use the sewing machine in conjunction with any two-dimensional research to further develop design concepts.

Project preparation

Many fashion designers have a signature to their collections, which is synonymous with their label. Once you become more proficient with your sewing techniques, you will start to develop a more individual, creative approach to your work that will reflect your design aspirations. This chapter will introduce you to the basics of sewing techniques, and will guide you through the initial stages of understanding the sewing process.

Confidence is the key to progression: it allows the designer to creatively explore complex sewing processes. Within this chapter, sewing terminology, machine operation and basic practical exercises will be introduced, offering a guide to sewing techniques.

Essential equipment

Garment and sample engineering requires various different types of sewing equipment depending on the designer's needs and the scope of the project. This section provides information to help you identify the equipment easily and progress through the book. It also includes information on the type of equipment to use to record the processes, which is essential to designers who like to reflect on each stage of their work. However, use your discretion: if you find a piece of equipment that does the same job better, use it.

1.4
Basic sewing equipment
Basic equipment should include fabric scissors, paper scissors, chalk, tape measure, seam unpicker and a magnetic seam guide. Pins are an option but beware: if they are caught in an industrial sewing machine, they can cause damage.

Lockstitch machine

There are many industrial sewing machines available, many of which may look slightly different, but do not be daunted, most of them thread up in very similar ways. It does take some practice to be able to thread a machine correctly but it will take you a matter of minutes once you have mastered it. Threading instructions may be found either on the machine or within the manufacturer's handbook. Lockstitch machines do vary slightly according to the different manufacturers but they all perform the same function.

Thread tension gauge

It is essential that the sewing machine is threaded correctly to ensure that it functions properly. A significant area that is often overlooked is the thread tension gauge. This gauge allows the top (the thread that is positioned on top of the machine) and the bobbin to work in harmony by allowing equal amounts of thread to travel smoothly when sewing. The thread tension gauge consists of two discs between which the thread is inserted, as well as a dial that enables you to adjust the tension as needed. When done correctly, sewing can proceed without any problems such as loose thread or puckering of the fabric.

After completing the 'threading up' process, test the machine by using a spare piece of fabric. Start sewing, check the stitches and adjust again if required.

Serger/overlock machine

Overlockers are designed to neaten the raw edges of the fabric, including seams. The machine has a blade that cuts off a minimal amount of fabric, which is then overlocked using several threads. Sergers perform the same process; but are a little more versatile in that they can also be used to coverstitch seams (mainly stretch or jersey fabrics) and to chain stitch (used in the construction of jeans).

There are two-, three- and four-thread overlockers, each denoting the number of threads used on the machine. These are used for different types of fabric:

Two-thread overlocker
Used on silks or delicate fabrics that require minimal handling.

Three-thread overlocker
Used to overlock the edges of woven and heavier fabrics that have a tendency to fray.

Four-thread overlocker
Used to form a seam. Rather than using a lockstitch machine for sewing knitted or jersey fabric, this stitch allows the thread to stretch with the fabric.

The instructions for threading these industrial machines can be found on the machine or in the manufacturer's handbook. Tweezers are used and you will need a lot of patience to complete the process. Do not feel daunted when undertaking the task: it takes a little practice but persevere.

Differential feeds

Sergers/overlockers can appear to be quite complex pieces of machinery but one of the main components is the 'differential feed'. This means that the feed systems can be adjusted to work at the same speed or one can move a little slower or faster than the other. These feed systems can prevent puckering, such as when overlocking a raw edge, to ensure that it remains flat. They can also provide more decorative effects, depending on the setting. Sergers are great for creating decorative edge finishes such as a lettuce hem (which resembles the edge of a lettuce leaf) and can be adjusted manually.

Decorative edge finishes in the fashion industry are done by machinery specifically designed for the purpose. This is because it is time consuming and not financially viable to change the settings for the different finishes. Overlockers are often set to perform one function only: overlocking raw edges. They are adjusted using a computerized setting on the machine, often by a specialist machine technician.

Bobbin/spool and case

The two separate pieces are the bobbin, around which the thread is wound, and the case, into which the bobbin is inserted.

A = bobbin/spool

B = bobbin case/spool case

A

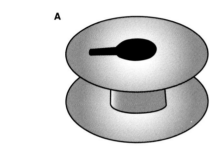

B

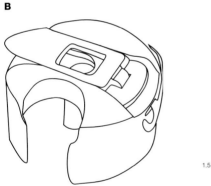

1.5

Bobbin/spool and case

Bobbin/spool – for industrial machines, this is often made from metal. It is cylindrical in shape and the bottom thread is wound around it.

Bobbin/spool case – the spool is inserted into this metal case that controls the tension of the thread.

When the bobbin is inserted into the case, the thread is slid through a little opening that leaves a small excess of thread. This is then inserted into the sewing machine; however, this must be executed correctly as it may cause some damage to your needle if not. On most industrial lockstitch machines it is inserted horizontally; check before inserting. It should be easy to insert but you might have to use a little pressure; you may hear a clicking sound that indicates you have inserted it correctly.

This thread is used to loop around the top thread when you bring the needle down. When you bring the needle up, it will bring the bottom thread with it and both threads will be visible on the plate of the machine.

Mechanism – bobbin/spool and case

Before a bobbin can be inserted into a spool case, there are several procedures to follow.

Ensure the machine is switched off. Take an empty bobbin and fill it with thread, which will ensure that the thread is smooth and able to run through the needle without any problems. There will be a mechanism to do this on the machine that is operated by the treadle. Ensuring that the presser foot is in the raised position and the machine is threaded correctly, press the treadle. On most machines as soon as the spool is full the winding motion will stop automatically; however, always check this because you do not want the spool to overfill as this will cause the thread to tangle and problems with the stitch will occur.

Once this is complete, take the bobbin and unravel no more than 5cm (2in) of thread, then place the bobbin into the case. Take the excess thread and pull this through the thread slot on the bobbin case. Now place the bobbin into the machine.

With the presser foot lowered, thread the sewing machine, ensuring that the needle is threaded.

Lower the needle into the throat plate, as far as it will go. The top thread will automatically pick up the bobbin thread from the bobbin hook to form a loop. As the needle is raised, both threads will appear on the throat plate. They can then be pulled through, so that you have two even lengths.

Always test the machine prior to sewing.

1.6

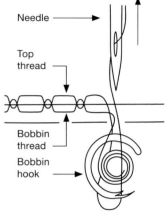

Needle

Top thread

Bobbin thread

Bobbin hook

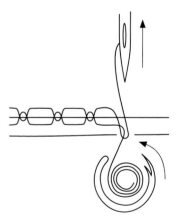

Lockstitch machines are one of the most common machines used in the production of fashion clothing. The stitching mechanism is controlled by foot using the treadle/pedal, which makes the machine start and stop when and where required. Lockstitch machines are useful for different weights of fabric as they have interchangeable feet, including some that apply pressure to the feed dogs to give stability when using heavy fabric.

The lockstitch seam is a straight stitch, which provides a smooth professional-looking finish to a garment. It is particularly used to sew woven fabrics together and is found in some of the following places: armholes, side seams, hems, cuffs, and collars.

The lockstitch can also be used for decorative purposes such as top stitching, and free machine embroidery.

1.8

'Create your own style... let it be unique for yourself and yet identifiable for others.'

Anna Wintour

1.8
Marios Schwab, F/W 2012
Sewn using a lockstitch machine, this embroidered bodice has soft raglan shaped sleeves and neck pleats.

1.9
Dries Van Noten, S/S 2006
Cream jacket with pillar-box red collar, worn with deconstructed dress. Both would have been sewn using a lockstitch machine.

1.9

Lockstitch needles are used for sewing woven fabrics. They produce a straight stitch, the length of which can be adjusted according to requirements. The needle has a standard point, which refers to the sharpness of the needlepoint, and comes in different sizes.

1.11
Lockstitch foot
A lockstitch foot is also known as a walking foot. It is used to sew basic seams and comes in different weights for different types of fabric.

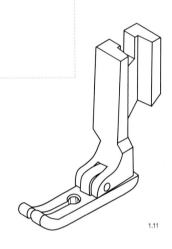

1.11

1.10
Lockstitch needle
Example of a lockstitch needle.

Lockstitch foot

All machine feet should have guards on them to prevent any accidents during the sewing process. Also known as standard feet, they are universally used on all lockstitch machines. They are attached and secured to the machine by a screw; when changing one, ensure that it is very tight because if it becomes loose, it can damage your work and cause an accident.

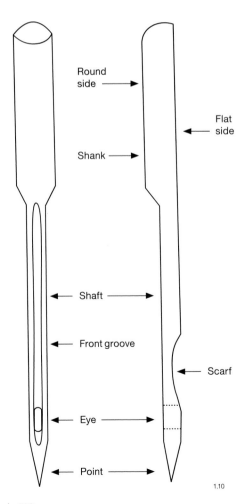

Round side

Flat side

Shank

Shaft

Front groove

Scarf

Eye

Point

1.10

1.12
Concealed zip foot
A concealed zip foot is wide
and short as shown in the
illustration and has a hole in the
centre where the needle inserts
itself during operation. This
provides a space between
the zip edge and the teeth.
Jeans have concealed zips.

1.13
Invisible zip foot
The invisible zip foot can get
close to the teeth of the zip.
When the zip is inserted into
the garment, it appears to be
invisible in the seam, giving
the garment a clean and
uncluttered finish.

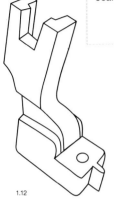

1.12

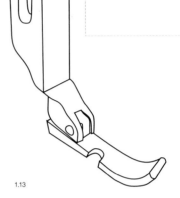

1.13

Concealed zip foot

A concealed/lapped zip foot is specifically designed for the insertion of concealed zips. It is normally held in place on an industrial sewing machine by a screw, which should be secured before sewing. When inserting a concealed zip, it is important to use this foot for the correct finish; you can of course use a lockstitch foot but the zip may be uneven when complete.

Concealed zips are topstitched once they have been inserted. This finish can be seen on skirts and trousers alike.

Invisible zip foot

An invisible zip differs from a concealed zip in that it is often slimmer and you are unable to see the teeth as they are concealed by fabric. The zip pull and centre seam are the only visible elements. The invisible zip foot differs from the concealed zip foot by its width; it is noticeably slimmer and has a half moon-shaped insert. This insert allows the stitch line to be sewn as closely to the edge of the zip as possible.

When constructing the invisible zip, you will need a left and a right foot; this will mean changing them to complete each operation. If you try to use one foot for sewing both sides, one side will be uneven and when the garment is worn, you will see the actual zip rather than a seamless line. Invisible zips can be found in dresses, skirts, trousers and other garments.

1.14

Depending on the type of fabric you use and how the garment will perform when worn, there are several different types of threads available. The most popular are cotton and polyester.

Cotton threads are matt, with very little sheen. When a garment is worn and washed over time a cotton thread will become weak. However, it is widely used in ethical clothing, if it complies with ethical growing guidelines.

Polyester threads are synthetic; they are very economical and used in mass produced clothing. They can be either matt or sheen and the colour does not fade easily. In addition, they are very strong.

1.14
Sewing threads
Expensive silk threads are good for sewing silk as they share the same composition. They are very soft and tend not to knot, which is advantageous when sewing delicate fabrics. Metallic threads are sometimes used for decorative purposes; however, due to their thickness a needle with a large eye should be used.

Activity 1: Basic seams

Plain seam

At first, sewing a straight or curved line can be tricky. If it helps, draw the line first, and then practise.

A seam of 1cm (0.39in) is a standard seam width in the fashion industry. This is the most common seam type that can be found on clothing, such as the inside of skirts, trousers and blouses.

1.15
Plain seam
This plain seam has a seam allowance of 1cm (0.39in); when you first start, practise with a 2cm (0.78in) seam, then reduce it as you gain confidence.

A

Place right sides together, ensuring edges are placed evenly on top of each other. Sew a 1cm (0.39in) seam. Make sure that you secure the stitch by pressing the bar tack bar at the beginning and end of the row of stitching to prevent the thread unravelling.

1.15

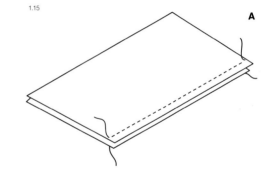

A

B

Press open the plain seam to complete. If you are confident, try overlocking the edges but be very careful to avoid damaging the seam.

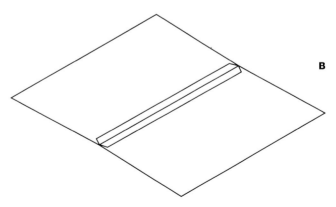

B

French seam

French seams are used on very delicate fabrics where overlocking is not suitable, such as silk chiffons that have a tendency to fray.

1.16
French seam
This diagram of a French seam shows that the raw edges are enclosed to give the inside of the garment a professional finish.

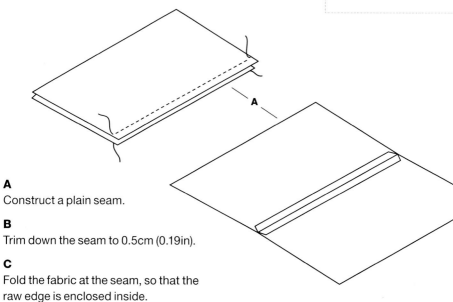

1.16

A
Construct a plain seam.

B
Trim down the seam to 0.5cm (0.19in).

C
Fold the fabric at the seam, so that the raw edge is enclosed inside.

D
Topstitch (sew) both pieces of fabric together 0.6cm (0.23in) from the edge of the folded seam.

When this is complete, there should be no raw edges visible on the inside of the seam.

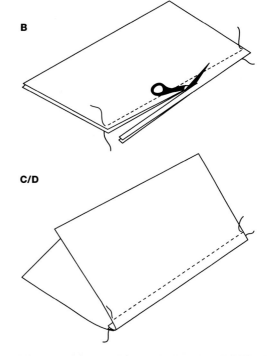

Flat fell seam

Flat fell seams are found on the inside legs of jeans. This seam is used because it is very durable and conceals the raw edges.

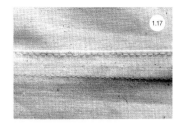

1.17

A

Construct a plain 1.5cm (0.59in) seam and trim the bottom layer by 0.5cm (0.19in).

B

Fold the upper seam allowance over the trimmed seam, ensuring that it is folded over the raw edge.

C

Press all layers flat and topstitch (sew) both pieces of fabric together 0.3cm (0.12in) from the edge of the folded seam.

When this is complete, there should be no raw edges visible on the inside of the seam.

1.17/1.18
Flat fell seam
The flat fell seam is similar to a French seam except it is stitched flat to the base of the fabric and is used on heavyweight fabrics such as denim.

1.18

A

B

C

The image shows three areas that may be troublesome when sewing, but with a little patience and practice, these can be tackled with confidence.

A: Uneven overlocking

To prevent this, overlock in stages by stopping and starting the machine throughout the process. This will prevent the seam being pulled into the machine too quickly, which can cause damage.

B: Uneven seam

There are several ways to achieve an even seam. Adjust the machine settings so that it is slower, allowing you more control of the machine. Alternatively, draw the line with chalk and use it as a guide when sewing.

C: Overlocked overlocking

This is often noticeable when the operator has been unable to control the machine and the overlocking is not sewn along the edge of the fabric correctly. It often leaves a very unsightly finish. Overcome this by regularly practising your overlocking techniques.

1.19
Troubleshooting
This plain seam shows several areas where problems may occur: overlocking, seam construction and uneven seam width. Each of these problems is easy to correct.

1.20
Uneven French seam
This French seam is uneven, which usually occurs when the seam allowance is uneven or the seam is pressed unevenly.

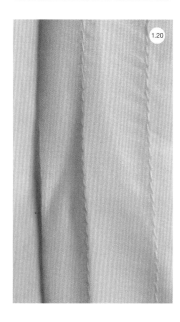

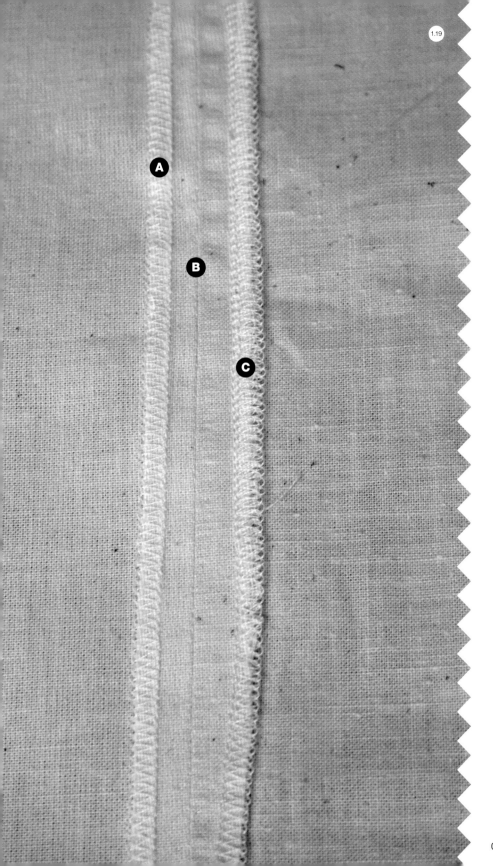

Mada Van Gaans' creativity took flight at the Vrije School (Rudolf Steiner college) in Meppel and Groningen, Intermediate Technical School for Fashion and Clothing MTS in Utrecht, and the Amsterdam Fashion Institute. She received her final Masters from the Fashion Institute Arnhem, where she presented her graduation collection at Musée Galliera for Haute Couture Week in Paris. She completed internships with Renate Hunfeld, Beach Life, Bernard Willhelm and Oscar Sulleyman.

In 2001, Van Gaans was selected for the Robijn Fashion Award. She presented herself internationally by participating in the design contest ITS#3 Talent Support in Italy, and took part in several exhibitions in Paris, New York, Rome, Barcelona and London in collaboration with the Dutch Fashion Foundation. In the Netherlands, she exhibited her clothing in museums such as Gem in the Hague, the Museum of Modern Art in Arnhem and Historical Museum Amsterdam.

Mada premiered her collection at Amsterdam Fashion Week in 2005. The same year Mada went to New York City to show her collection during New York Fashion Week, and took part in the exhibition 'Dutch at the Edge of Design' at The Museum at FIT. In 2007 Mada was nominated for the Dutch Fashion Awards and came second in the IAF Awards in Taipei, Taiwan. In 2008 Mada was nominated for the Dutch Fashion Awards for the second time.

She has been commissioned to design unique pieces for the international Lavazza calendar campaign photographed by Erwin Olaf and a series of limited edition 'Belle Arti' watches for Longines. She designed two collections with Just B.

Her work is refined and detailed, with a whimsical and art nouveau touch.

Strong formations, softened by flowing materials and elusive prints are brought together within a dreamy, yet wearable, range of refined outfits suitable for modern women.

Natural elements and traditional craftsmanship from other cultures are placed in a new light and show how multicultural craftsmanship can work harmoniously with modern cloth.

1.21–1.28
Mada Van Gaans, Serpent Goddess collection, F/W 2010
The delicate fabrics, forming soft pleats, tucks and gathers, add an ethereal quality to the collection.

1.21

1.22

1.23

Where do you get your inspiration?

I get my inspiration from the art nouveau period; I like to look at the drawings, painters, artists, furniture and fashion designers from that time. Also traditional clothing or rituals from other cultures. I like to explore tales and myths about gods and demons and female figures. Other inspirations are movies from the 1920s through to the 1970s, visiting exhibitions and travelling. Also elements from out of nature, shapes and colours of plants and flowers, colour combinations in birds or reptiles, bugs or creatures that are living in the sea.

To me, it is a challenge to be able to translate the rich images and silhouettes from those magnificent artworks into my creations.

Do you believe the creative process involves all aspects of garment realization?

It's an important starting point to create new shapes and colour combinations; next to that it's very important to know the technical skills of pattern making, sewing and how to finish the clothes. It is also important to know what it is comfortable to wear, which you will learn out of experience and by trying on lots of clothes in the shops.

You also have to know what will suit each body shape; there are a lot of different body types. For one person a V-neck is the best option and for another a round turtle neck.

When do you consider the types of sewing techniques you intend to use within your collections?

I look at the kind of fabric I use and the price level of the garment. For chiffon silk dresses, I prefer the French seam finish; the hem has to be very small or I use a small satin baby lock. If the garment is more casual, you can also use a mouse stitch lock. In jackets, for example, you can choose total lining, half lining or just bind the seams, it all depends what you like to show with the piece. The inside is very important, especially in the high-end brands.

How much time do you spend considering sewing techniques within the creative process?

Most of the time is spent on this part of the job, which is why it is important to be skilled in it. A good designer, in my opinion, has to know how to make and finish clothing; otherwise, you cannot explain what you want to the production department. You can study this at college, at home or take a separate sewing class.

When visualizing the finished collection, do you think trims/notions are an important feature?

Yes, they are very important; the machines you work with have to be good, and the yarn and notions you use will make the job cleaner and easier. Ironing is also important, and to iron the clothing parts between every sewing step. It will make a big difference in how the clothes look.

How important is sewing within the garment realization process?

Important; you have to know how to make a piece of clothing in order to tell others what you want.

What types of fabrics do you like to use?

Silk chiffon, Jacquard woven fabrics, cotton/silk blends, silk chiffon with Lurex woven patterns, summer wool, wool with cashmere, fancy fabrics with structure.

What is your advice for new designers?

To practise a lot with different fabrics, to see what will be a good finish. To shop a lot, try on clothes in the shops, look at the shape, feel the fit, and look at the inside as well as the outside of clothes to examine the finish. Buy second-hand clothes and tear them apart to see how they are made; this is interesting with jackets or asymmetric, bias-cut dresses.

'To me, it is a challenge to be able to translate the rich images and silhouettes from those magnificent artworks into my creations.'

Mada Van Gaans

1.25

1.26

1.27

MADA VAN GAANS

1.28

2

Preparation

2.1
Research
Strong, architectural-inspired research informs the finished details of the
coat design; the strong lines, colours and trims are all prominent features.

Design interpretation

There are many different approaches to design interpretation and everyone develops their own individual technique. However, a very simple starting point is to make a copy of your drawing (this will be used as a template) and label each component (see example). Within each square, identify the different areas; for example, what type of neckline or armhole does it have? What type of seams do you want to use? Does it fasten at the back or the front and what type of fastening is it?

Does it need a facing? Initially, you could write these elements as a list, then you can start to do a rough sketch of the garment only. At this stage, you could produce a pencil drawing. Most designers scan these into CAD applications to complete the working drawing to a professional standard.

2.2
Sketches
A designer makes notes and thumbnail sketches to assist with the construction details of the collection.

2.2

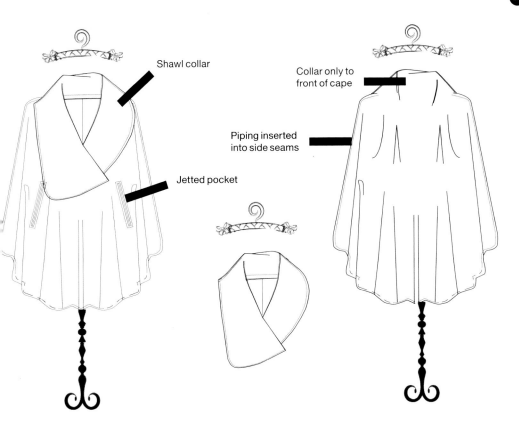

Shawl collar

Collar only to front of cape

Piping inserted into side seams

Jetted pocket

Working drawing

A working drawing, also know as a croquis or technical drawing, is an accurate interpretation of the designer's illustration of both the back and front views of the garment. This enables the designer to identify exactly how the garment will be constructed and any design details, such as notions/trims, pockets, collars, sleeve type and so on. It is also essential for communicating design information to sample rooms, factories and anyone involved in the product development process.

2.3
CAD drawing
A CAD working drawing identifies components that will be sampled before the toiling process takes place. This helps the designer to determine the correct size and shape and to establish which sewing techniques will be required.

Crucial measurements

For garments to fit correctly, accurate body measurements should be taken. Although this varies slightly from retailer to retailer, the terminology and measuring process is similar. This information is often included on a chart with the working drawing so that the garment can be produced to fit. However, this should not be confused with a garment size chart, as these are produced by pattern cutters to help them create pattern with 'ease' to allow for styling, comfort and fit.

The crucial measurements for the female form are the bust, waist and hips. Obviously, there are other measurements that need to be taken into account but the focus, for ease of understanding, will be on these three areas.

Using a tape measure and mannequin, measure the following areas and record them.

A: Bust – Place the tape measure around the mannequin at the fullest part of the bust. Record this measurement.

B: Waist – Place the tape measure around the mannequin's waist at the slimmest part. Record the measurement.

C: Hips – Place the tape measure around the hips, the widest part of the mannequin. Record the measurement.

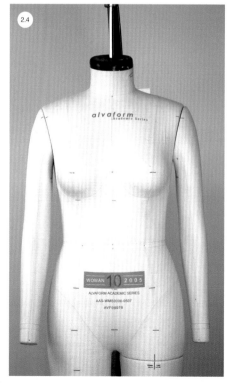

2.4
Mannequin
This female mannequin benefits from having detachable arms; these are very easy to remove and are useful for fitting samples with sleeves.

2.5
Elie Saab, Haute Couture, F/W 2009
This beautiful fitted organza dress is elegant and serene.

2.7
Fitting process
A student determines where
to insert darts into a bodice
by placing the toile on the
mannequin and following the
natural lines at the waist.

Importance of fit

The measurements you have recorded
are not clothing sizes, these are the sizes
used to determine a pattern for a garment.
A pattern cutter will then add 'ease' to
these measurements (ease is the numerical
difference between the body and garment
points, allowing room for fit and movement).

Within the fashion industry fitting a garment
occurs over several stages, which enables
amendments to be made until the desired fit
and look is achieved. In many cases, this is
called the 'sealing process', and can consist
of the garments being measured 'flat'
(placing them flat on a table and measuring
against a garment size chart specification
to determine whether they have the correct
measurements). In addition, the garment
can be fitted to a 'fit model' (see Chapter 5
for further information).

Note taking is essential at this stage, in
order to make any necessary amendments
and to assess the fit of the garment before
adding any features. The designer should
focus on the critical areas and consider the
following (based on a bodice):

Neckline: is it too high/low? Alternatively,
is it too tight?

Armhole: is it too high/low or too tight?

Bust/chest: is it too tight/loose?

Bust darts: are they in the correct position?

Waist: is it in the correct position? Is it too
tight/loose?

At this early stage in the development,
the designer has the opportunity to change
any styling detail and reassess the overall
look of the garment.

2.6
Jean Paul Gaultier
In fit sessions with his model
to check the fit and finish
before the runway show.

Creating shape within a sample can be in the form of pleats, tucks, darts, etc. Clever use of these details can greatly transform the silhouette of any garment, making a collection more interesting and recognizable.

An advanced technique of introducing shape to a garment is by shrinking the fabric. It is mainly used in tailoring and on fabrics that are 100% wool or wool blends as they tend to shrink or stretch easily due to the fabric composition. The process involves applying a steam iron to the fabric then removing the steam and using only heat. This will result in the fabric shrinking and is particularly effective when removing fullness at the waist or bust.

Shaping can also be in the form of seams and tucks such as the Princess seam which is shaped to create a fitted silhouette through the bust and waist points.Tucks vary and range from a tight cluster of overlapped fabric to pintucks, which are narrow folds of fabric securely sewn into place with rows of stitching. Pintucks are often a decorative finish found on children's clothing.

However, one of the most commonly used sewing techniques is darts, which are stitched folds of fabric that taper to a point (see Darts on page 44 to see some of the different types). These simple additions allow the garment to fit closer to the body to accommodate the natural shape of the figure. Generally, it means taking out the excess fabric where it is not needed and positioning it in an area where it is, such as at the bust.

Adding darts to a garment is not only a practical way to reduce volume, but also makes it more comfortable for the wearer. Equally as important will be the overall aesthetic finish.

2.8
Marios Schwab: Runway – LFW, F/W 2012
Neck darts have been inserted into this bejewelled high neckline to give a defined shape to this sheer outfit.

Dart positions

Darts can be used as a decorative as well as functional feature. Some designers use them as design features to contribute to the overall theme of their collections.

The process of moving darts, in which darts can be repositioned or completely closed, is known as dart manipulation.

Darts can be positioned in the following areas to accommodate the body shape:

Front bodice – bust point

Back bodice – shoulder blade

Front skirt – centre of hip

Back skirt – buttocks

The two main methods of dart manipulation are:

Pivoting – this is where the block is 'swung' to close, open or reposition a dart (see example for transferring the shoulder dart at the underarm). This method is more accurate and used widely in the fashion industry.

Slashing – the block is traced, the new dart position marked on the block, then this is cut to allow the other dart to be closed. The finished block will have a dart in the new marked position.

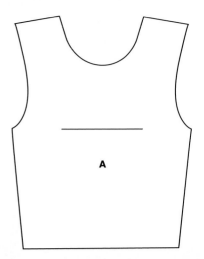

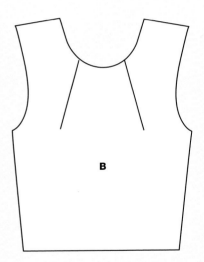

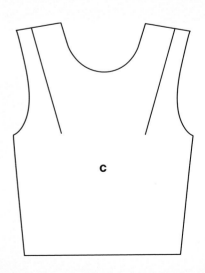

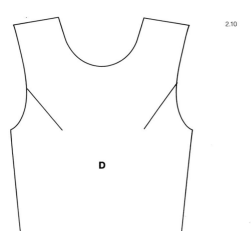

2.10

2.9/2.10
Dart manipulation
Each of these bodices
shows how darts have been
manipulated using pivoting
or slashing according to
design requirements.

A = Bust dart

B = Neck darts

C = Shoulder darts

D = French darts

E = Waist darts

F = Centre-front chest darts

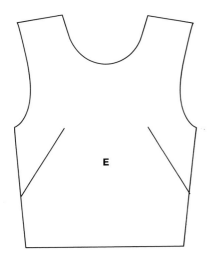

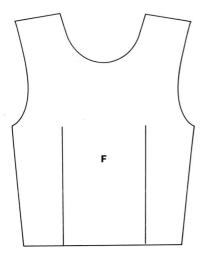

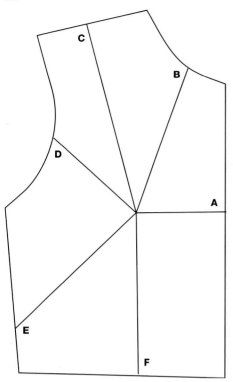

2.11
Darts on the bodice block
Each line on the bodice
indicates where the darts are
inserted. They meet in the
middle at the bust point.

Dart types

Female bodice block showing the position
of each dart:

A Bust dart

B Neck dart

C Shoulder dart

D French dart

E Waist dart

F Centre front chest dart

2.12
Marios Schwab, S/S 2012
Dart types A, B and F have
been used on the bust and
neckline on this layered, sheer
fabric bodice.

The type of fabric used for the sampling and garment process should be chosen to replicate your designs. If a heavyweight fabric is required for an autumn/winter collection, for example, try to find something similar, if not the actual fabric. This allows time for the designer to consider the elements of the sampling process, such as the colour palette, the theme of the collection, the handle and drape of the fabric. If the creative vision of the collection is to be realized, sourcing the right fabric is key. To eliminate some of the problems that may arise during fabric selection, contact the fabric supplier. Many of them provide small swatches, so that their suitability can be assessed.

Woven fabrics

Woven fabrics can come in many weights, from light through to medium and heavy. Most are made from natural fibres, such as cotton, silk and linen but are also available in synthetic mixes. They are often very durable and can be cut and sewn easily as they have little natural stretch.

Cotton calico is often used for sampling and toiles (test garments); it is fairly inexpensive and allows the garment to be fitted and amended before it is made out of the final fabric. However, be aware that cotton calico is not suitable for all sewing projects, particularly where close fitting garments are to be produced, and a stretch fabric may be more suitable. If cotton is used for a sampling project ensure that it is pre-shrunk before you cut out your pieces.

If the cotton is not pre-shrunk and the sample or garment is then pressed or laundered, it will shrink and cause problems with fit and size.

Wool is a popular woven natural fibre. It is often mixed with other natural and man-made fibres, which can provide more durability to a garment. Wool retains heat and is a common fibre in outerwear (coats and jackets). Sheep's wool is the most common type; however, there are others such as alpaca, angora and cashmere, which are very luxurious, popular and expensive alternatives.

Silk fabric is a natural fibre that comes in many different finishes; it is breathable and therefore keeps the wearer cool in warmer climates. Silk takes dyes very well but at times the colour can vary according to the quality of the dyeing process. Silk organza is lightweight and sheer; it has to be handled with care due to its delicate nature. Dupion silk is slightly heavier than silk organza and features irregular slubs (a slightly raised appearance), which adds to the richness of the texture.

2.13
**Basso and Brooke,
F/W 2010**
Graphic printed silks and
jersey fabrics are a bold feature
of this collection.

Knitted fabrics

Knitted fabrics have more stretch in them
because they are knitted rather than woven
and can be produced from natural or
synthetic fibres, or both. Lightweight knitted
fabrics are used in lingerie; heavier weight
knits are used in sportswear and casual
wear as they provide comfort to the wearer.

2.14
Lining fabrics
Polyester linings are available
in a variety of shades and
weights but you can also find
lining fabrics in silk and cotton.

Lining and interfacing

Interfacing is used to stabilize and
support fabrics; it can be found in collars,
cuffs, jackets, waistbands, and so on.
It is available as woven and non-woven;
some types are available with adhesives
that stick to the fabric when heat-sealed
and others can be sewn in. Before using
interfacing, always assess its weight
to ensure that it is not too heavy or light
for your chosen fabric.

Lining fabrics are available in natural or
synthetic fibres; they are used in jackets,
coats, trousers, skirts and dresses.
Lining provides a professional clean
finish to the inside of a garment and
conceals raw edges, interfacings and
garment components.

Pressing and steaming

Garments and samples are pressed with an iron to smooth away creases and wrinkles and also to press flat seams and add creases, such as trouser or skirt pleats, collars and cuffs, and so on.

For an unfinished garment in a toile state, 'under pressing' can be done, which is the process of pressing the components rather than pressing the entire garment at the end of the process. The equipment should be in good working order and set to the correct temperature. It is also important that you know how to use it correctly and safely. This is where knowledge of the composition and finish of the fabric is essential.

The pressing station will consist of an iron and a vacuum table to hold the garment in place, so that if you apply steam whilst pressing, you are able to depress the vacuum pedal with your foot to draw the steam away. It will also have arms, which are used for pressing sleeves and collars.

2.16
Steaming
The delicate pleats would lose their form if they were pressed flat; they have been steamed to retain the fluidity of the dress.

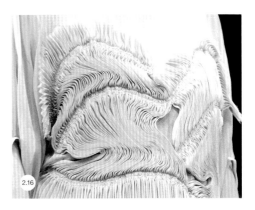

2.16

Some natural, delicate fabrics such as silk chiffon react more positively to steaming than ironing. This is mainly because, if an iron is set to the incorrect temperature or setting, the fabric risks being damaged by heat or by watermarks (if steam is used).

Steaming (or steam treating) is the use of steam (hot water vapour) to remove wrinkles or creases from clothing. This piece of electrical equipment consists of a cylindrical canister and a steam distribution handle. Water is placed in the canister and heated to the correct temperature. Once this is complete, steam will appear from the handle and garments can be steamed in the hanging position, rather than flat.

2.15
Reem Acra, S/S 2005
Elegant permanent pleats have been inserted into this calf-length skirt, giving both structure and movement to this garment. Specialist equipment has been used to ensure that these permanent pleats do not lose their shape.

Sample folio

The sampling portfolio is a reference point for any designer; it offers the freedom to experiment without restrictions and to develop creative ideas that can work in conjunction with the second stage of the design process. The sample folio can form part of the design research and development process. The ideas within this can simply be sewn samples that replicate an image from the mood or concept board. At this stage, it is about exploring design possibilities through three-dimensional practice.

There are no mistakes during this stage and in most cases, the designer is able to enhance or develop new concepts that may not have arisen through the sketchbook process. Sewing does not have to be perfect; this can be perfected when the designer is at the toile stage and, even then, any mistakes can be rectified.

2.17

2.17
Reviewing processes
Once all of the visual references have been acquired, it is an ideal time to review the creative processes undertaken to get to this stage. It may be that the designer wishes to add or remove some details. Placing all the images together, spread out on a table or pinned to a board, for example, provides a platform on which to reassess or refine the creative process.

Documenting

When documenting the process, the designer should try to take as many notes as possible. These could be in written form, or be thumbnail sketches, magazines and newspaper cuttings. They should be anything that can inspire the creative sampling process. It may seem like a jumble of information but this process enables the designer to understand in depth the final look and feel. When constructing the samples, assess whether you get the required effect, through hand or machine sewing, to replicate an image from the mood or concept board.

2.18
Sampling
Images of the sampling process sit nicely together with fabric samples and working drawings or sketches to provide a reference point for the designer.

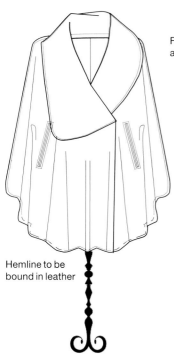

Fuse front facing
at centre front panel

Cape
Structured shoulder line
All raw edges to be bound
Two buttons to secure
coat on inside

Hemline to be
bound in leather

Shawl collar
to be interlined

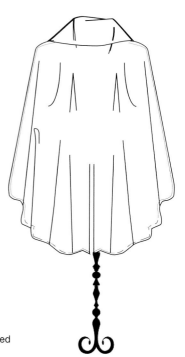

Recording

Recording the process can simply be by sketching or through the use of photography and video. Recording something you are making and viewing it later can provide new, exciting insights, which can lead to advanced creative sampling. Consider the light, which has a profound effect on how things are viewed, and these impressions can be translated back into samples.

Recording can also involve the use of CAD packages and uploaded photographs and video. These packages allow for further experimentation. CAD functions such as layering, distorting, filtering and so on, add a new and unexpected dimension to the recording process, which can then be used to develop further sampling.

2.19
Working drawing
This working drawing consists of component parts that the designer has highlighted as important features for sampling. Clear notes explain the types of finishes, such as trims/notions, and how these will affect the overall silhouette.

2.20
Hellen Van Rees, 'Square One: The Miracle of the Space Age' collection, F/W 2012
Natural tweed fabrics take the shape of sculptural three-dimensional forms that add a modern touch to a classic look.

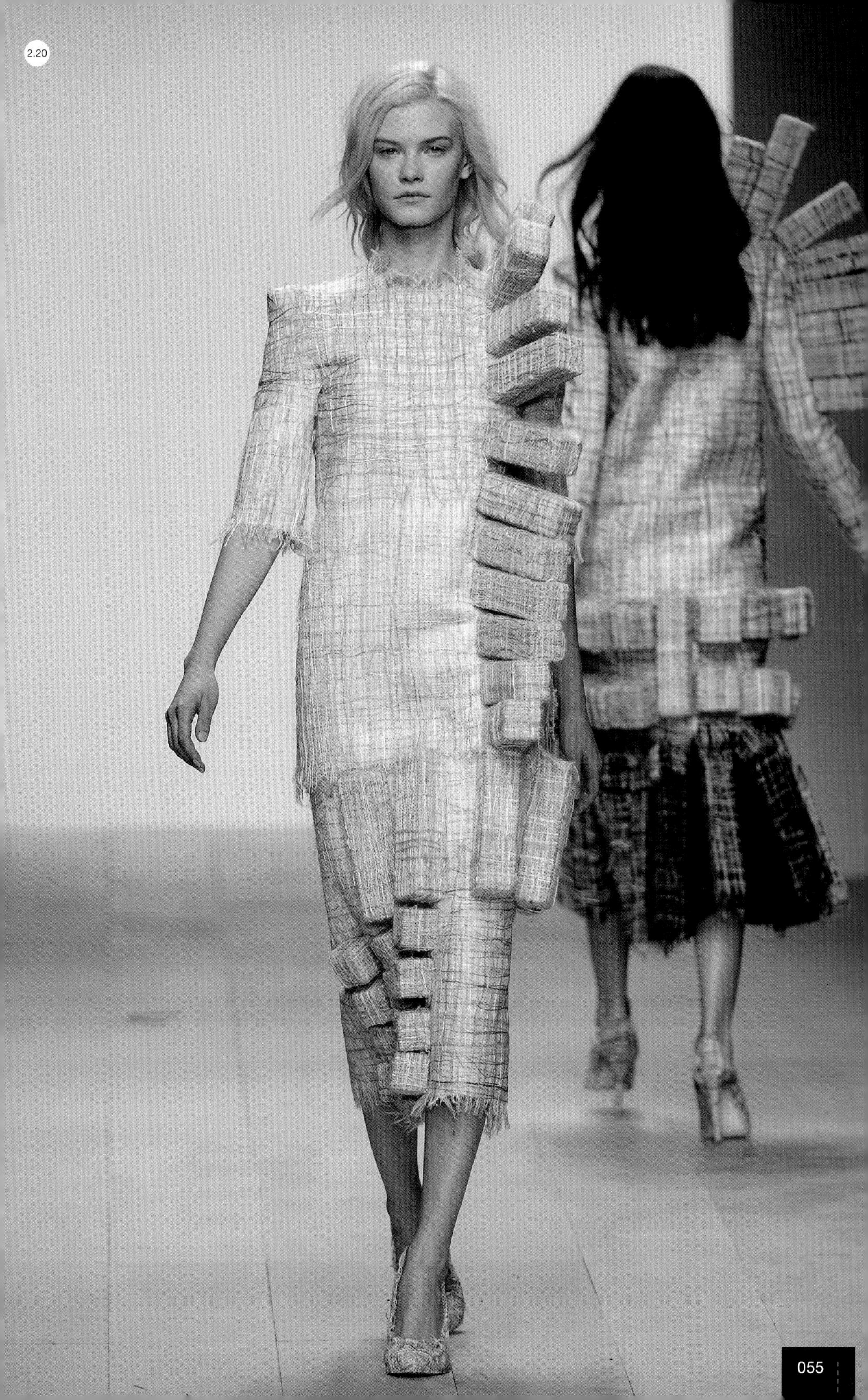

2.20

Sewing corners

When sewing corners, there can be the tendency to sew to the end of the fabric, then to sew another row of stitching that intersects this. Although this may be acceptable for the sampling process, if it is undertaken at the toile or final garment stage, it could result in the garment being damaged after the seam has been trimmed down because the threads are no longer secure.

Needle control will not only eliminate this problem but will also help with controlling the machine.

A
Lay the fabric on a flat surface with the right side facing up.

B
Place the right sides together.

C
Using a seam of 1cm (0.39in), start sewing but only sew a few stitches and press the reverse pedal on the machine to secure the stitches. When you reach the first notch, stop, DO NOT lift the needle up, leave it in the fabric. Lift the machine foot and pivot the fabric in the direction of the next line. Put the foot down and continue sewing, repeating the process until you have completed three sides. Remember to secure the stitches at the end.

D
Take a pair of scissors and snip the corners of the two edges; trim the seam down. Turn through to the right side and press.

2.21
Sewing a corner
These instructions demonstrate how to sew a corner, with the needle remaining in the fabric at all times.

A = The two sections of identical fabric, side by side

B = The layers on top of each other

C = Stitching to two sides and with the corners cut

D = Completed sample, turned through to the right side

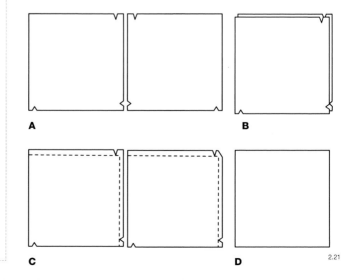

A

B

C

D

2.21

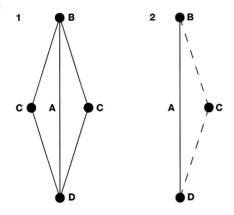

2.22
Sewing fish darts
The diagram shows the points from which to sew the fish darts. Starting at the top, reverse the stitch to secure the thread and avoid it unravelling. Also secure it at the end.

A = fold

B = top of the dart

C = centre of the dart

D = bottom of the dart

1 – Dart marked on the fabric.

2 – Fold the fabric down the centre of the dart.

Fish darts and waist darts

Ensure that the centre dart points are matching.

Start sewing from point B, secure the stitches as previously and sew down at an angle to point C.

When you reach the first point C, stop, do not lift the needle up but leave it in the fabric. Lift the machine foot and pivot the fabric in the direction of the next line. Put the foot down and continue sewing just past point D, not too far. Finally secure the stitches at the end and press the dart towards the side seam.

Now try to sew image 2.23.

2.23
Sewing a waist dart
The diagram shows the waist dart when it is marked on the fabric. Once it is folded, start to sew at the top and reverse the stitch to secure it. When you get to the end of the dart sew over the edge of the fabric slightly, then reverse the stitch to secure it.

A = waist

B = width of the dart

C = foldline

D = bottom of the dart

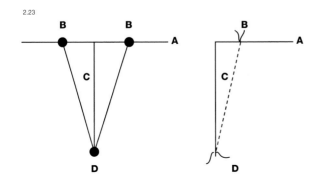

Activity 3: Curved seams

Sewing a curved seam

Curved seams are used for a variety of components, such as collars, cuffs, pockets and so on. This sewing technique demands a certain amount of control to gain the best visual effects. There is a lot more to consider when sewing this shape: not only do you need to be accurate, but the curve needs to be finished smoothly. That is, unless a more irregular shape is required.

In preparation for this task use half-moon shaped pieces of fabric rather than a complete circle, until you gain more confidence. Start by sewing slowly and do not worry about securing the edges.

A
Place the right sides of the fabric together and start sewing at the top notch. Reverse the stitch to secure it.

B
Carefully and slowly, match the edges up and ensure that the notches B match up. Continue sewing (but DO NOT overlap the fabric as this will distort the seams), until notches C are matched. Continue sewing to the end and reverse the stitch to secure.

C
Using fabric scissors, snip V-shaped sections out of the seam, being careful not to cut into the seam. This allows for the curve to stretch into its natural shape.

D
If required, trim the seam down and press open.

2.24

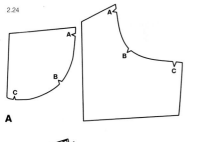

A

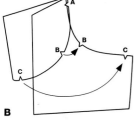

B   C

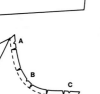

D   E

2.24
Sewing a curved seam
These instructions for a curved seam show how the fabric should be pivoted so that the raw edges meet and remain even as they are sewn.

A = The two sections side by side

B = Both fabrics together

C = The first section of stitching

D = Completed sample, edges snipped

E = Finished sample, flat to demonstrate curve

2.25
**Qui Hao, Serpens
collection, F/W 2011**
Quilted, topstitched collar
in satin-like fabric.

When trying to solve any problems with the sewing, first check that the machine is threaded correctly. Ensure that when threading the needle the foot is in the raised position, it is a lot easier. Check the bobbin/ spool, if it is threaded correctly; is the excess thread correctly positioned in the thread slot and does it move freely when you pull the thread? If not, adjust the 'lower thread tension screw' (the thread should not be too loose or too tight but should be able to move easily). Is the correct bobbin/spool inserted? If you are in a studio environment where there are different models of sewing machines, do not swap the bobbins; this can cause thread tension problems and ultimately damage to any sewing project.

Problems with tension can arise because of the tension discs, which control the amount of pressure used for the top thread to sew even stitches. If they are either too tight, causing the machine to unthread, or too loose, causing the machine to sew loose stitches, then adjust the dial accordingly.

Sewing curves can be quite tricky. Trying to match two opposing curved edges has the potential for the seam to become puckered and unattractive. To avoid puckering, slow the machine down (depending on model, the speed is adjusted by a dial located underneath the machine). This will provide more control and allow for the notches to be matched correctly, resulting in a smooth, professionally finished seam.

Darts can pose a problem, they can be uneven in length when finished, can be puckered at the bottom. If you experience either of these problems, as stated previously, adjust the machine so that it is slower, when you reach the bottom of the dart, ensure that the last stitch overlaps the edge of the fabric and reverse the stitch to secure it, running it along the edge of the fabric. When you press the area, do not stretch the garment over the board, as this could distort the shape.

Remember, all sewing techniques require practice.

2.26

A – unpressed seam
The topstitched edge along the curved pocket is not flat near the side seam; this is due to not pressing the seam evenly before topstitching. Ensure this is pressed before sewing.

B – roping
The seam along the curved pocket is known as 'roping'. Roping is a term used when a seam leaves a raised impression in the fabric when it is topstitched. To eliminate this, ensure that the seam is snipped correctly or trimmed down enough to reduce the bulk. Once this is done, the seam can be carefully pressed flat before finishing with topstitching.

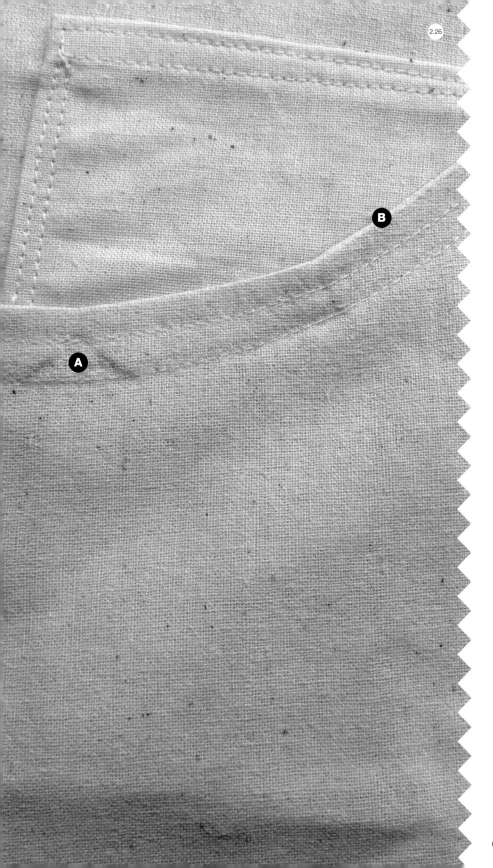

Ada Zanditon, born and based in London, is a first class graduate of the London College of Fashion. Ada Zanditon made her London Fashion Week catwalk debut in September 2009 (Fashion Scout, Ones to Watch). Core to the brand philosophy is a sustainable business practice, which Ada is constantly refining and seeking to improve. A wide range of sustainable textiles are sourced. This is part of her design philosophy, a belief in the strength of diverse systems.

Where do you get your inspiration?

My inspiration comes from a scientific perspective on the environment, modern architectural forms and a blending of historical journeys with future fantasy. I am also inspired by the process of evolution and the concept of biomimicry and I try to be innovative through mimicking the process that has evolved in nature.

Do you believe the creative process involves all aspects of garment realization?

Yes, we believe that the creative process is involved in every aspect of garment realization, from design to the finished product. All the design, the technical and the sustainability aspects are considered in our creative process.

How are your sustainable and ethical practices translated throughout your collections?

From the ground up we try to approach sustainability as practically as possible. The ways in which we do this start with the materials and fabrics we use, the processes in which we manufacture and the way in which we communicate our message about the brand. We communicate our message creatively and we try to make this as engaging as possible.

The mission of the brand is to engage a mainstream audience through fashion, who may not typically be aware of sustainability.

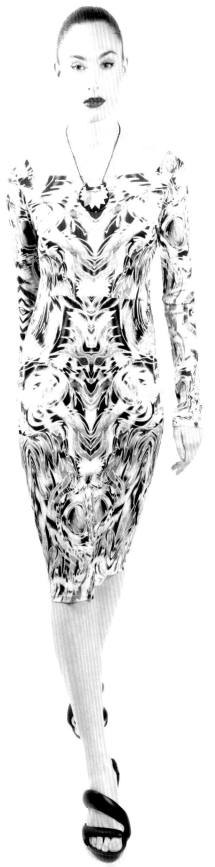

'The mission of the brand is to engage a mainstream audience through fashion, who may not typically be aware of sustainability.'

Ada Zanditon

2.27–2.29
**Ada Zanditon,
'March of Tigress'
collection, F/W 2013**
Conservation-inspired
collection produced with
ethically sourced fabrics.

What amount of time do you spend considering sewing techniques within the creative process?

It would be hard to quantify exactly how much time, however when we create any garment it is a core part of the creative process. We always like to make sure we are getting the best result and we do this by initially making our samples in the studio, before taking them to be manufactured in the factory – this is to guarantee that they are at the standard we wish for them to be.

When visualizing the finished collection, do you think trims/notions are an important feature?

I think trims and notions are a very important feature, therefore we prefer wherever possible to create our own. As we create very innovative and unique products, we try to create the majority of trims and notions from scratch, as they are hard to source otherwise. We consider this to be an important aspect of our design process.

How important is sewing within the garment realization process?

This is essential; the quality of our stitching is of the upmost importance and it is very crucial that it is correct. We hand finish our bindings and many details on the clothing both inside and out, so not only is our stitching important – but also our hand finishing. I feel that this makes our garments both high quality and unique.

What types of fabrics do you like to use?

We use a wide range of innovative sustainable materials, including fair trade organic cotton, bamboo, Tencel, aluminium, silk, recycled wood, end-of-line materials and British wool that is woven in Yorkshire.

What is your advice for new designers?

My advice to new designers is to have a strong business plan, a clear idea of who your customer is and what your unique sales point is. It is also important to deliver a product that you are passionate about, as it may take a number of seasons before you have good sales and press. Therefore, it is important that it is something you really love doing, in order to engage with people through your brand.

3.1
Clasp closure
The clasp on this dress is purely for aesthetic detail;

Closures

Creative statements can be made with the clever use of closures. This can be seen across many fashion collections and can have an enormous impact. They can be anything, from a button to a zip; be used for practical or decorative purposes, can be subtle or blatantly obvious. Whatever is chosen should be selected with consideration for the fabric type, garment, and overall aesthetic finish.

Selecting a zip or zipper will depend on its usage; considerations should be made for heavyweight or lightweight fabric and the zip chosen accordingly.

Take time to source the zip, so that you are able to experiment with the different insertion techniques. Also, take into account whether the zip is purely for aesthetic reasons or function and performance. Most zips come in metal or plastic. There are also zips that are produced for waterproof clothing and are made of a synthetic material, which allows it to be bonded (glued or heat-sealed) to the garment rather than sewn.

Invisible zip – when constructed, these zips are hidden within the seam. The stitches are not visible on the right side of the garment; therefore, they are good for dresses and skirts, where clean lines are the required finish.

Concealed zip – often seen on jackets, trousers, jeans and skirts. This is where the zip is concealed by a guard and topstitched. It comes in both heavyweight and lightweight types and can be used decoratively.

Two-way zip – coats, parkas and sportswear feature these zips. They are designed to open completely and have two zip pulls for ease of use. Most often, these are heavyweight and are available in both metal and plastic.

3.2
Invisible zip
Invisible zip inserted into a seam, then topstitched as a design feature.

3.3
Yohji Yamamoto, S/S 2006
Invisible zips have been inserted into the front of the jacket, used to hide or reveal the garment underneath.

Buttons and buttonholes

Buttons are one of the oldest closures, dating back to the Bronze Age. They were originally used as decorations; they were later used on clothing. They can be found in both natural and synthetic materials. Buttons can be finished in very decorative patterns or can be quite plain; vintage ones can be sourced if required and they are very simple to make. They come in a variety of shapes and sizes but as stated previously, if the intention is to make an impact, try to source these at the design stage as it can sometimes take a long time to find the right style for a collection.

Buttons are available in a wide variety of materials, such as plastic, metal, wood and shell. Most are circular in shape but square, oblong and triangular shapes are also available. Some buttons have holes, others have a shank (a small hook attached to the back of the button). Shank buttons are often used on very heavy garments such as overcoats, as they allow movement when the garment is worn.

Buttons are one of the most common closure options, yet they are the most interesting. There are just a few points to take into account:

Always match the thread colour to the garment, unless you want a contrasting finish.

Lightweight and heavyweight buttons should be matched to a similar fabric. This is because a lightweight button will not be stable enough for a heavyweight fabric and vice versa.

If you are matching buttons to fabric, ensure that you have a swatch to match them against.

Do not be afraid to experiment with different button types, such as covered buttons, leather and metal.

Always consider the button size before buttonholes are inserted, as it is difficult to rectify this once it has been done. Ensure that they are evenly spaced by marking the button position first. Also consider the width of the buttonhole, it needs to be wide enough to accommodate the button but not too wide. As a guide, 3mm (0.12in) wider than the button is adequate.

3.4
Street style, day 2, Milan Fashion Week, S/S 2013
Blogger Chiara Ferragni wearing an azure silk Giorgio Armani high-neck dress. The decorative finish to the front of the dress gives the impression of flowers and could also be used to disguise any button fastenings.

Buttonholes

Horizontal – coats, jackets and cardigans have horizontal buttonholes; they provide good stability to any areas of stress at the opening of a garment.

Vertical – shirt and blouse plackets are normally very slim so vertical buttonholes are more suitable; again, for stress purposes but also for discretion.

Keyhole – this resembles a keyhole at one end and normal buttonhole opening at the other. It was traditionally used for very heavyweight garments and can accommodate movement between the button shaft and the hole.

Bound – the raw edges of the buttonhole are encased in strips of fabric, which can either be self-fabric or contrast.

'To me, clothing is a form of self-expression – there are hints about who you are in what you wear.'

Marc Jacobs

3.5
Bound buttonhole
Double-breasted leather jacket, complete with bound button holes and a shank button.

3.6
Keyhole buttonhole
Machine finished keyhole buttonhole.

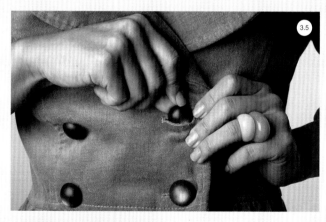

3.5

3.6

3.7
Ann Demeulemeester, F/W 2009
Utility style jacket with zip and hook-and-eye detail to collar. This hook-and-eye detail is noticeable rather than discreet.

Hooks and eyes and press studs

Generally, hooks and eyes come in different shapes and sizes, whereas press-studs are the same shape but vary in size.

Always mark the position where they are to be attached. This is so that the closure parts line up correctly. When attaching them to the garment try not to sew through to the other side, as this will be visible.

The most stable are metal hooks and eyes; these are solid metal and are suitable for waistbands where a lot of pressure will be applied.

Round hooks and eyes are very delicate and are mainly used as a closure for dresses at the centre back neck point.

Press studs, also known as snaps and poppers, are disc shaped and form the closure with one section inserted into the other. These two sections are called 'male' and 'female'.

They are attached to the garment using a 'press'. This piece of equipment applies the correct amount of pressure in order to ensure that the press studs stay in place and do not damage the garment. When attaching press studs, ensure that you mark the position accurately as the male and female studs need to be aligned correctly.

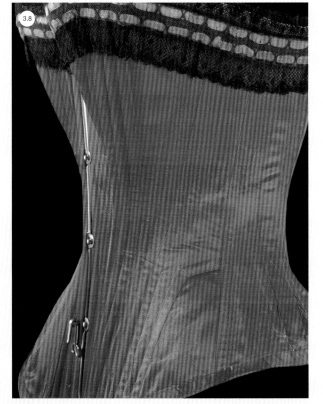

3.8

3.8
Corset, V&A Museum
The Victorian and Edwardian hourglass shape was formed by this type of corset with hooks and eyes attached to the front.

3.9
Jean Paul Gaultier,
F/W 2013
Model wears skirt with a press stud opening and fitted jacket, with the press studs being used on the bodice to highlight features.

Reviewing the process is an ideal time to reflect on your own practice. You may wish to consider whether your design ideas are being realized in the way you expected. If they are not, consider how to change the process in order to develop them. It may mean that you reassess and change some of the approaches to developing the sample portfolio. This could be in the way in which you are approaching certain elements, for example, are you producing sample after sample or are you developing that sample to try to create something different?

Use this time to question your process and try to extend your ideas beyond the sketchbook to create something fresh and exciting.

Refer to your sample folio: is there anything that you can improve? Have you documented the processes correctly? Is there anything you would like to change? Have you been experimenting with some of the samples? If not, try to experiment with some of these techniques.

3.10–3.12
Student portfolio
This student portfolio is being used to develop the sewing techniques. A dress has been selected and a sketch has been drawn to show how the garment functions and where the details will be placed during the experimental phase. The mannequin displays a toile the student has developed; at this stage, all elements of the design and realization process can be reviewed, ensuring that the information is documented for future reference.

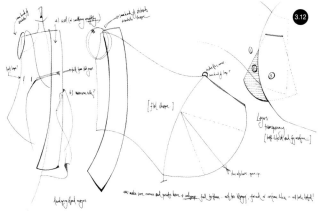

Activity 4: Inserting a zip into a seam

Inserting a zip is a skill that needs to be practised. The first time you do this you may not achieve perfect results but keep trying. The key is to have patience, but the most important thing is to have the correct zip length for the opening of your garment; if it is too long, then have it shortened. Ensure that you have the correct foot or feet (refer to page 21) and that it is fitted correctly and test the lockstitch machine by sewing on a spare piece of calico or fabric. If the machine speed needs to be adjusted, do so. To build your confidence you can hand sew the zip into the correct position before sewing but try not to use pins to hold it in position. Pins can severely damage a lockstitch machine if used during the sewing process, particularly if they snap or get caught in the machine.

Insertion of zip: Part 1

Clean lines and minimalist finishes can be achieved using this method. It does take practice but the results add a level of sophistication. You will need the following:

× Invisible zip (any length)

× Two pieces of calico fabric (approximately 10cm (3.93in) longer than the zip length)

× Invisible zip foot.

Image 1

× Place one side of the zip face down on the right side of the fabric.

× Place the zip foot as close the teeth as possible, secure the stitch and sew. Stop at least 2cm (0.78in) from the bottom of the zip.

× Repeat this for the other side.

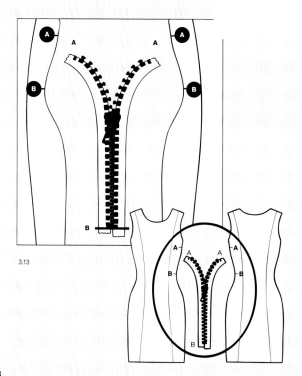

3.13

3.13
Inserting a zip
This illustration shows how a zip is inserted into the side seam. The top of the zip is placed level with the top of the fabric.

Key

A = Top of the zip

B = Bottom of the zip

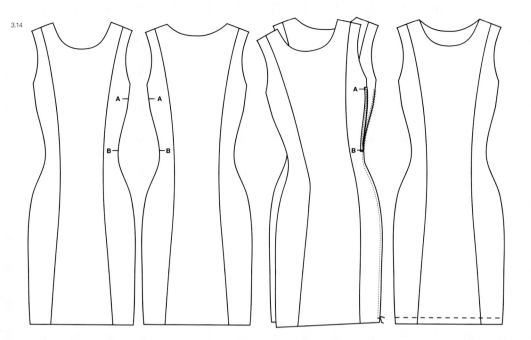

3.14

Insertion of zip: Part 2

You will need the following:

✕ Lockstitch machine foot.

Image 2

✕ Change the zip foot to a lockstitch foot.

✕ Place the right sides of the garment together at the zip side seam.

✕ Starting at the hem, use a seam allowance of 1cm (0.39in) and sew the seam up to the opening of the bottom of the zip.

✕ Complete the garment by sewing side seam and both shoulders with a 1cm (0.39in) seam allowance.

3.14
Inserting a zip
The diagram shows how to insert a zip into the side seams. In this case, it is an invisible zip, with the side seams being sewn together after the zip has been sewn in.

Zip insertion can be problematic particularly at the top where the zip pulls. If problems are encountered here pull the zip down before sewing, so that the zip is open, then begin to sew. This will avoid the zip pull being visible when the garment is finished and will eliminate any uneven stitches at the top of the garment.

With any zip insertion, when complete, check that the zip can be pulled up and down with ease. The issues to be aware of with an invisible zip are to ensure that you sew close enough so that the fabric part of the zip is not visible (when complete it should look like a continuous seam) but it should not be sewn too close to the teeth as this will prevent the zip from working correctly. A concealed zip normally has problems at the top where the pull is. You may find that the stitching will be uneven in this area; if it is, make sure you have followed the instructions on page 78, and pull the zip down so that it is open before construction.

On the right side of the seam, the zip is visible. To rectify this, unpick the zip and the seam. When you place the zip foot, ensure that it is as close to the teeth as possible. The foot should sit just under the teeth.

On the wrong side of the garment, the seam is visible. This is normally due to lack of machine control when sewing. To avoid this, try sewing the zip in stages, stopping (with the needle in the fabric) to check that it is straight before proceeding.

3.15
Right side of sample
Is this invisible zip insertion, on the right side of the seam, the zip is visible. This indicates that the zip is not sewn close enough to the seam. To rectify this, ensure that the zip foot is as close as possible to the zip teeth.

3.16
Inside of sample
On the wrong side of the seam, the edge of the seam is clearly visible and uneven. To avoid this, try sewing the zip in stages, in a 'stop/start' motion. It is simply a case of stopping to check at each stage of construction.Ensure that the needle and foot are in the correct position, and then continue to sew. By completing this in small steps an accurate invisible zip will be achieved.

Jonathan Jepson is a London-based fashion stylist with clients throughout London and Europe. In 2012, he graduated from De Montfort University, UK, with a BA (Hons) Fashion. On completing his studies he was offered a place at the London College of Fashion to study for a Masters but decided instead to enter the industry and gain experience. Jonathan has since gone on to work for the high street and designers such as Burberry and Ozwald Boateng.

Where do you get your inspiration?

I draw inspiration from a number of sources; my general inspiration for my graduate collection focused around death and the loneliness in which our souls are cocooned. Memento mori photographs often feed into this source of inspiration and lead to the investigation of textures and fabrics as opposed to actual silhouette design. Music from artists like Antony and the Johnsons or Keaton Henson to me evoke fully the feeling of fear and loneliness and the general vulnerability we all have to our own emotions and state of mind.

Do you believe the creative process involves all aspects of garment realization?

Personally, design and realization of the actual garments and the looks of the finished collection don't start to form until after I have figured out the direction and mood I want to create. Sometimes this can be as late as the initial pattern cutting stage.

3.17–3.19
Jonathan Jepson's menswear collection
Luxe sportswear with black dominating each piece. A mixture of knitwear, polyurethane and silks make up this collection.

When do you consider the types of sewing techniques you intend to use within your collections?

I figure out the sewing techniques while pattern cutting or when I find the fabrics I intend to incorporate into garments; it's a constant thought process as patterns and fabric selection change.

How much time do you spend considering sewing techniques within the creative process?

The time spent considering sewing techniques, as with any consideration needed for design, depends on the length of time set out for the collection. Generally, I will consider which techniques fit best for the garment through the initial and final toiling stage. Once a final toile is made there shouldn't be any need to reconsider seaming and stitch detail.

When visualizing the finished collection, do you think trims/notions are an important feature?

Visualizing final finishes and trims, for me, only happens when I am happy that the fit and silhouette of the garment are right. Then I consider the buttons, trims, zips and so on, add these to the final toile, then evaluate.

How important is sewing within the garment realization process?

I think that sewing and the techniques you intend to use are massively important, the wrong seam on a fabric can not only change the quality of the garment but also the aesthetic of the finished piece, especially how it drapes or hangs on the body.

'...don't let rejection get you down, fashion is about perception: one brand could hate your work but another one will love it.'

Jonathan Jepson

What types of fabrics do you like to use?

The fabrics used in any collection really do depend on the source of inspiration and the mood of the collection but I gravitate towards luxury fabrics such as furs, leathers, exotic skins, silk chiffon, fine laces and silks mixed with more resilient sport-focused fabrics like Partex, silk jersey and always 100% cotton for men's shirts.

What is your advice for new designers?

The only advice I could give to anyone venturing into this business is learn to network! Don't be the quiet, shy person in the corner, no one remembers those people; get involved in the conversation, you never know who you could meet or what could come of it. In addition, don't let rejection get you down, fashion is about perception: one brand could hate your work but another one will love it.

4

Professional finishing

4.1
Contemporary menswear tailoring
Striking menswear illustration for Brioni collection by Dan WJ Prasad.

All collections demand a tremendous amount of creative work behind them. Some designers have a full team that assists with everything from sourcing fabrics to creating collections; others and particularly new designers are involved in most or all of the aspects and become immersed in developing a collection.

We learn from the designers that the creative process involves all aspects, in that two- and three- dimensional design processes are not separate but that both need to be combined in order for design evolution to take place. This involves the reassessment of original goals, revising and refining them.

In this chapter, we explore the ideas behind collections, from research ideas to sample development and beyond. The creative skills needed to develop concepts are translated through fabric, surface manipulation, embellishments and garment realization. The designers in this chapter have provided a rare insight into the inspiration, process and development of their collections. Their interviews are personal accounts of how they created signature styles, the meanings behind them and how they have been interpreted.

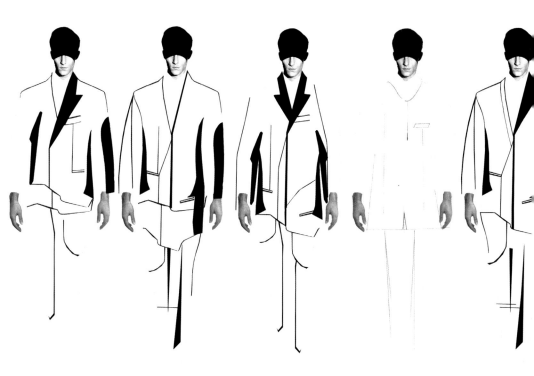

The interviews demonstrate how the designers challenge their own processes; try different techniques and experiment in order to keep evolving the design. Their experiences of traditional sewing techniques, including hand sewing, are covered in this chapter and although the roots of these construction techniques are historical, they have been brought up to date with a modern, contemporary twist. In addition, fabric selection is discussed and how fabrics can be used to create silhouettes, features and creative themes.

Canadian graduate Yvonne Lin provides a personal account of her inspiration, which translates through to contemporary and timeless smocking and slashing. Emma Hardstaff presents impressive silhouettes, that demonstrate the creative skills required to manipulate fabric using sewing techniques to great effect. Designer Funmilayo Deri's elegantly structured collection evokes a feeling of mystery and Louise Bennetts' striking architecturally inspired collection takes traditional to a different level. Finally, the international designer Elie Saab provides a case study about his life, creative inspiration and elegant haute couture collections.

Through these insights you will learn that inspiration can be found anywhere but it requires an experimental and open-minded approach as well as the conviction to believe in your work.

4.2

4.2
Dan WJ Prasad, 2013
Brioni Menswear
Award Winner
Brioni Collection final line-up
redefining traditional
menswear tailoring.

Yvonne Lin graduated from Ryerson University in 2012, with a Bachelor degree in Fashion Design. She was the winner of the 2012 Who's Next Prêt-à-porter in Paris, as well as the undergraduate ITAA Target Market Award, Hawaii, and the Theo Cokkinos Memorial Award and Frankie Landau Apparel Design Awards, both in Toronto.

Where do you get your inspiration?

FORMATION is an art to wear collection inspired by Michael Hansmeyer's 'Ornamented Columns'. Michael Hansmeyer, a Zürich-based architect and computer programmer, uses algorithms to transform abstract Doric columns into complex pillars with multiple divisions of their facets. 'The columns are about nine feet tall, weigh about 2000 pounds, and are made out of 2,700 1mm-thin slices of cardboard stacked on top of wooden cores, containing between 8 and 16 million polygonal faces' (John Smith described the exhibition in Pavlus magazine in July 2010.). Both architectural detail and design method/process provided inspiration.

FORMATION adopted the production idea of the columns by using plain white fabrics and transforming them into three-dimensional forms. Columns were viewed as emblematic of the complexity of life. A hand-smocking technique was chosen to reflect the symbolism of reunion and separation, and a 3D leather slashing technique created a wavy effect that was used to convey the idea of the ups and downs in life. Traditional hand techniques and innovative pattern drafting were combined to create a stunning art form in itself. The outfit is structured yet soft without over-sexualizing the female form. The collection spoke about contemporary women with a balance of femininity and toughness.

4.3/4.4
Dress detail
White, calf leather slashed
dress with close-up of detail.

4.5
Bamboo top
Bamboo textured top with
long sleeves. The sharp pleats
are also extended through
to the high-waisted skirt.

Do you believe the creative process involves all aspects of garment realization?

For the FORMATION collection, I used a very different design approach than before. I started with just sketching something abstract and then figured out how to reach the idea. Before that, I thought very technically rather than creatively; I would only design what I thought I could construct. It kind of limited me in my design. The new design process was much more interesting and more challenging, since it involved taking something abstract and making it into something concrete while still conveying its meaning to an audience. As a student, it was more fun to explore something unknown than repeating what you already knew. Therefore, I would recommend students to push their creative boundaries. However, when going into the industry, I do think we always need to keep both creativity and marketability in mind. I have to admit, that is the most challenging part to me, and I am still learning to find the balance between both.

When do you consider the types of sewing techniques you intend to use within your collections?

It came together when I had the inspiration and theme for the FORMATION collection. Smocking and 3D slashing were the two main techniques used. The collection was inspired by Michael Hansmeyer's work but also by a story of my own. Being raised in the very rural countryside of southern China, I have to admit I found city life hard at first. Unlike the countryside, everything is so fast-paced in a city. So I decided to do an art to wear collection, which is considered very time consuming to produce, to speak about this idea. I like to work on one thing for a long time; I feel by doing so the work/products have more personality attached to them, and a stronger bond between wearer and designer.

Smocking techniques represented reunion and separation in life. To explain further, the way of creating smocking was by plotting dots on a garment (just like our paths in life) and by pulling specific dots together and separating the rest, a pattern was eventually formed. Just like in life, we meet with new people and separate from others as life goes on.

Exercise

Describe Yvonne's inspiration. Can you see how her research has been translated? How has she used the slashing technique? How has the shape been developed?

Slashing was used to indicate the ups and downs in life. These little instances later shape who we are as individuals. Each experience, no matter how good or bad, leaves some kind of marks in our life. Eventually, life is not just as simple as a plain piece of fabric, it gets complex. Everything started as white, but the different texture and depths create light as well as shadows, which is also what makes life so interesting. The collection is not just a story about me, but also represents what I try to remind myself; no matter what is ahead of me after graduation, I have always to be brave and face it.

How much time do you spend considering sewing techniques within the creative process?

Lots, it took time to experience and explore. For most design students in the fourth year, studio was our home. We spent most of our days in there. Funnily enough, our lab number is 247, which matched what we were doing in there, 24 hours a day and seven days a week. Everyone got closer because that was home for most of us. Of course, there were also tears and stress, but the passion kept us going no matter how hard it was. When you saw your work on the runway, and heard comments from other people, you felt everything paid off.

4.6
Bamboo top
Bamboo textured top with slashed leather trousers.

Bamboo dress
Bamboo dress with textured
bodice panel, pleated sleeves
and open back.

4.7

When visualizing the finished collection, do you think trims/notions are an important feature?

I do think every detail is important. I did
not use many trims in my collections.
The predominant detail was the zippers.
The zippers for dresses ran longer than the
dresses themselves, leaving around 4-inch
tails. They were exposed and stitched
directly on the outside of the dresses. This
technique was inspired by Givenchy's 2011
couture collection. The zipper created
an illusion of a spine, which, in my opinion,
added interest to the collection.

How important is sewing within the garment realization process?

To me, sewing is a very important part.
It is like everything else, you can only get
creative and innovative when you have
a strong foundation, and sewing is what
I consider to be one of the foundations for
fashion design.

What types of fabrics do you like to use?

When I choose a fabric, I like to touch it.
The hand of a fabric is very important to me.
I would say I have preference for organic
and matte fabrics, such as cotton, wool and
silk chiffon. Chiffon is such elegant fabric,
and it really tests your sewing skills. Yet it is
a fabric that cannot be substituted by other
fabrics. For the FORMATION collection
I used bamboo jersey for the smocking
tops. This was to stop the finished garments
wrinkling, since I could not iron the
smocking after it was done. The pants are
stretchy denim and the major part of the
collection is leather.

What is your advice for new designers?

There is so much to learn. That is also
a question that I ask myself a lot after
graduation. But I would say you need
passion and hard work to be in this industry.
Fashion design most of the time is not
as glamorous as it looks but let's not forget
its very glamorous side, which is what
attracts many of us to this industry.

Where do you get your inspiration?

Inspiration for a collection can really come from anywhere. I try to start with something I am drawn to: a photograph, a film, a place; anything that inspires me to be creative. It is important to be aware of what other creative people are doing around you; I find it helpful to go to exhibitions and artist talks. I try to picture what I want to achieve from a collection, the customer I would want to reach and the showcase in which I would like to display my work. I like to think of the whole picture from the beginning.

Do you believe the creative process involves all aspects of garment realization?

Yes, you must approach every step of the process with creativity. As a designer I am constantly striving to create something new and desirable; for this reason I try to push every aspect of the garment realization, from design to drape to cutting.

Emma Hardstaff is currently studying an MA Womenswear at the Royal College of Art, London, supported by the British Fashion Council. She previously interned at Marc Jacobs in New York. During her degree at Edinburgh College of Art, she won several competitions including the David Band Textiles Award and the Medusa Cut and Colour Award, Graduate Fashion Week 2012, as well as the Harvey Nichols Design Collective Award 2012 and the Mackintosh design project 2011. She was also one of three finalists to be shortlisted for the Innovation Award, Graduate Fashion Week 2012.

4.8
**False Impressions,
F/W 2012**
Softly structured coat with dramatic pleated waist. The pleats are irregular at the waist, which gives the garment a more relaxed silhouette.

When do you consider the types of sewing techniques you intend to use within your collections?

I try to consider the sewing techniques as early as possible in the development process. The way a garment is put together is very important and can really dictate the direction of a collection. My design work is often driven by construction techniques; I always try to develop original methods of garment realization.

How much time do you spend considering sewing techniques within the creative process?

My work is driven by experimentation, trying new techniques and methods of construction. This process is often very time consuming as it involves a lot of trial and error. It is at this stage that you must be patient; try all the different options so you know when you are progressing in the right direction.

When visualizing the finished collection, do you think trims/notions are an important feature?

A trim can be the element that adds luxury to a garment. It is very important to choose the right finishings for your work as it is these details that people will notice and be drawn to.

4.9

4.9
**False Impressions,
F/W 2012**
Elegant, gathered, fitted
wool dress.

4.10
**False Impressions,
F/W 2012**
Open, pleated-front jacket
with electric pink dress.

4.11
**False Impressions,
F/W 2012**
White padded coat juxtaposed
with a soft, delicate skirt.

Exercise

Write down the types
of fabrics you think
Emma has used for her
collection. Try to find
similar swatches and
start to develop a fabric
sample portfolio. Then
build on this and start
to collect fabrics for
your own collections.

How important is sewing within the garment realization process?

Well of course, it depends on what you are making. For example my most recent piece was a pleated, oversized denim coat. I developed a construction method that involved attaching the open pleats at every seam. For this particular piece I used a blanket stitch, all sewn by hand. The garment could not have been sewn on a machine because of the particular construction method.

What types of fabrics do you like to use?

I often create my own fabrics, working with base materials such as cottons and silks, transforming them into exciting and original textiles. I try to think of the fabric in a three-dimensional context, altering it in a way that affects the silhouette of the garment. This can be realized through techniques such as quilting, flocking, pleating and so on.

What is your advice for new designers?

Think about whom you are designing for, and what it is about your work that is original. After that, it is simply about hard work and determination!

4.12

4.12
Full-length coat
Emma's techniques of manipulating fabrics have taken her years to perfect and the effects are amazing. Pintucks are a technique you could practise to develop skills like Emma's; see Chapter 5 for sewing techniques.

Funmilayo Deri is a Nigerian-born, London- and Budapest-based fashion designer. Initially earning a degree in International Business, she went on to study at the Istituto Marangoni in London. She developed a passion for fashion from a very early age and was always surrounded by creativity, designing and making garments with her mother as a hobby.

In March 2011 she launched her fashion label Funmilayo Deri. Her collections have since been presented at Africa Fashion Week, New York, and Vauxhall Fashion Scout during London Fashion Week. The collections received positive recognition.

Where do you get your inspiration?

My design aesthetic is influenced by my mixed cultural experiences and exposure and is a manifestation of my eclectic background. Inspiration for collections can come from movies, theatre, museums, nature, my travels and people. I am also inspired by my emotions. When designing collections, I start by selecting a theme around which the collection will be based. The chosen theme will be based on what is going on around me at the given time, and steers me towards certain music, people and places. All of these ultimately determine the direction of the collections.

Do you believe the creative process involves all aspects of garment realization?

Yes I do, especially when trying to develop collections that are commercially viable. When designing I consider how feasible it is to make each piece. Creativity plays a part in the development and finalization of patterns, toiles and samples, when I combine different intricate shapes of materials and varying colours to develop unique pieces.

4.13
Dress
Elegant velvet dress with lace sleeves and shoulders. The success of sewing different qualities of fabric together depends on the technique used. In this case the sleeves and armholes have been bound together to form a seam.

When do you consider the types of sewing techniques you intend to use within your collections?

Sewing techniques are considered while the designs are being developed, after initial sketches have been done and while fabrics are being considered.

How much time do you spend considering sewing techniques within the creative process?

The amount of time varies depending on the complexity of the design and the type of fabrics to be used.

When visualizing the finished collection, do you think trims/notions are an important feature?

Trims and notions are extremely important. I would say that they should be considered on the same level of importance as the fabrics used. They make up part of the details of any outfit and I do believe details are very important.

How important is sewing within the garment realization process?

The finish of a garment is extremely important. Clothes should be as beautiful on the inside as they are on the outside. The sewing techniques applied emphasize this design principle. I think the sewing techniques employed give an indication of the quality of a garment and should therefore always be appropriate for the fabrics used.

4.14

4.14
Skirt
Long black skirt with textured, exposed sides; each section has been joined together using a lockstitch. Worn with silk top.

4.15
Dress
One-shoulder lace dress with natural panel. The dress has been sewn to a natural coloured bodice. This gives the impression that the dress is being worn without support, when actually the under layer helps to give the garment shape.

Sleeve finish
Funmilayo's sleeve is very sleek and professionally finished. Lace can be notoriously difficult to sew because it is not a solid woven fabric. One option for sewing a lace sleeve is to secure the edge with bias binding. You will only need a width of 1cm (0.39in), so that when it is sewn together it is not visible on the right side. This finish also has the benefit of concealing the raw edges of the lace. See Chapter 5 for sleeve insertion sewing techniques.

What types of fabrics do you like to use?

I like to work with a variety of fabrics. I believe the choice of fabrics can make or break a piece. I use embroideries, silks, leather and lace and like to juxtapose fabrics of different weights, textures and colours.

What is your advice for new designers?

To succeed in the industry, the basics you need are talent, creativity and an extreme passion for fashion. Having these will keep your drive up when challenges present themselves – and they do! Internships are very important. If you're looking to set up your own label, intern with designers who are newly established. This way you see what they go through and it prepares you for what you will need to do when setting up your own label. As well as being creative, you must have good business acumen. If you don't, find someone you can partner with who does. This will ensure you run a successful fashion business and are not just partaking in an expensive hobby. The fashion industry is not all glamour, contrary to what many believe. It requires a lot of work, commitment and investment – both financial and time.

4.16

Exercise

Do you recognize the links between the garments in Funmilayo's collection? Write them down. Where has she used the zip? What type of zip is it? Start to collect images of different types of closures; look for ones that have been used creatively and discreetly.

4.17
Jumpsuit
All-in-one jumpsuit with exposed zip and panel inserts. The seam at the waist gives the impression that the garments are separated.

Louise Bennetts graduated from Edinburgh College of Art, UK, with a BA (Hons) in Fashion Design in 2012. Louise was awarded the Andrew Grant Award for Fashion as well as the John L. Paterson Award for Design Innovation. She was also one of the finalists for the British Fashion Council Nicole Farhi Award 2012. Louise is currently studying for an MA in Womenswear at the Royal College of Art, London.

Louise states that her current design focus is about how a sense of narrative and process can be incorporated at a design stage, creating garments with a purposeful sense of openness, leaving space for their user.

Where do you get your inspiration?

For my BA collection, Flux, my main source of reference was a series of photographs I took in Siena, Italy, where you can read the historical story of change and adaptation undergone by the buildings that make up the city. You can see arcades that have been built, blocked in, windows added, doorways taken away. Instead of being ugly scars, each mutation was worn as a proud mark of sustained functionality and bore evidence of the real people who used and changed these buildings. I sought to build clothes using a similar process, glorifying the process of how it has been made and how it could change in the future.

Do you believe the creative process involves all aspects of garment realization?

For the Flux collection in particular, I wanted the garments to seem 'finished' at each stage of their manufacture, like the Siena buildings, so traditional finishing techniques, such as bias binding, were instead used as seaming and construction techniques. Much of the collection was designed by working directly with fabric on to the stand. It wasn't necessarily a case of sketching a design, drafting a pattern and making a toile, it was a much more alive, unpredictable process. In that respect, the whole process absolutely considered all aspects of garment realization.

4.18
Trousers and jacket
The sharp jacket and wide-leg trousers provide a structured silhouette.

When do you consider the types of sewing techniques you intend to use within your collections?

I consider it quite early, as I feel that all aspects of the collection – colours, fabrics, finishings and silhouettes – should sit together cohesively and so need to be considered right from the beginning. This was particularly the case with Flux, as so many of the fabrics are transparent.

4.19/4.20
Binding
Binding is used on sheer fabric to bring the theme of Louise's collection together. This was an intentional detail, following the lines of her architectural research.

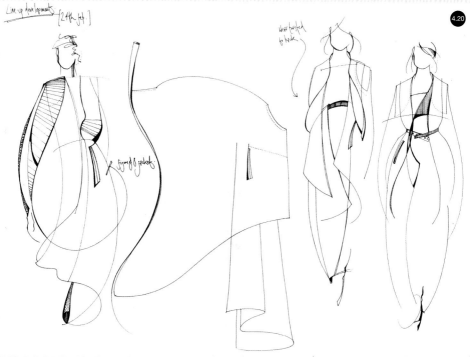

4.21

4.21/4.22
Fabric selection
The movement in the illustration is realized through the garment with a clever selection of fabric.

4.22

How much time do you spend considering sewing techniques within the creative process?

I knew I would need to refine the finishings so that the garments were beautiful inside and out (there would be no lining to hide behind!), so I invested a good amount of time into finding and perfecting the right techniques. I used a combination of bias binding (of various widths and made out of different fabrics), iron-on nylon flex material that cuts with a very clean raw edge, and sometimes even used the fabric's own natural selvedge. For the tailored pieces, the shoulder pads and padding inside the facings were made out of layers of tulle, to maintain the desired sense of transparency and 'exposed' construction techniques. My work is very concerned with the process of construction and 'building' clothes so I always try to showcase the techniques used to join fabric together rather than hide them away.

4.23

4.23/4.24
Sampling
The sample process is carefully undertaken, ensuring that the design research and philosophy is followed.

4.24

When visualizing the finished collection, do you think trims/notions are an important feature?

I think what makes a collection truly successful is often down to the finer detailing, so yes, even the smallest trim is something to be considered. I think if something has been designed with real attention to detail, the wearer will notice, and hopefully care for the garment more as a consequence.

How important is sewing within the garment realization process?

Similarly, I think the quality of construction makes a huge difference – student collections look immediately more credible and believable when made to a high standard. In addition, of course, the best-made garments are the most durable too!

Exercise

What type of industrial machine has Louise used to sew the binding on? Write it down. Try to sew binding onto the edge of a piece of calico. When you are satisfied with the finish, put this in your sample folio and try another one but using different fabrics.

What types of fabrics do you like to use?

I love transparent fabrics, as the way they are then joined together is so exposed, which is challenging but full of opportunity for interesting solutions. I also love building up layers, and transparent fabrics such as organzas and cotton organdies allow for a real sense of richness when layered on top of each other. I also enjoy using wool, as it is so mouldable and fantastic for tailoring. At the moment, I'm working with fabrics that perhaps have a more industrial aesthetic, such as canvas and felt, in an attempt to make them seem more luxurious through the application of refined sewing techniques.

4.25
Piping
A classic mixture of tailoring with a contemporary finish: binding. Louise has bound the edge to finish her garment, using bias binding. Another alternative is 'piping'. Piping cord can be inserted into the seam to provide a decorative finish. It involves placing the piping between seams and sewing it with an invisible zip foot, which will allow you to sew as close to the piping as possible. See Chapter 5 for the sewing technique.

History

Elie Saab was born in Beirut on 4th July, 1964, to a wood merchant and a housewife. Saab's interest in dressmaking started at the young age of 9. He spent much of his free time cutting patterns and drawing sketches for his sisters using his mother's tablecloths and curtains. The talent of this young boy spread rapidly through the neighbourhood, allowing him to create a small network of loyal clients.

He pursued studies in this field but quickly became bored, being a master already in the art of dressmaking and its know-how. In 1982, at the age of 18, Elie Saab opened his couture atelier in Beirut with a team of 15 employees.

In the following months, he presented his first collection to a public of young women who were immediately won over by the talent of this autodidactic artist, who soon became renowned for creating ultra-feminine dresses. His reputation rapidly transcended his country's borders, attracting clients from high society.

In 1997, Elie Saab was invited to take part in the prestigious Camera Nazionale della Moda as the only non-Italian designer, a true privilege. He showed his couture collection in Rome for three consecutive years before he was invited in 2000 by the Chambre Syndicale de la Haute Couture to show his collection in Paris. Every year thereafter, he has presented two couture collections in Paris.

Early career

In 1998, Elie Saab launched his ready-to-wear line during Milan Fashion Week, for the autumn/winter season, to rave reviews. The collection experienced tremendous success and garnered sales worldwide from Paris to Hong Kong.

In 2002, Elie Saab opened a couture house in Paris's eighth arrondissement to satisfy his cosmopolitan and international clientele, as well as a showroom presenting his chic and elegant ready-to-wear and couture collections to international clients.

4.26
Backstage at Elie Saab, Haute Couture, S/S 2013
Elegant models pose before the catwalk show.

4.27
**Elie Saab, lace detail,
Haute Couture, S/S 2013**
This dress would have
been finished by hand using
couture techniques.

The couturier

A few years later in 2005, Elie Saab
opened his new couture house in the heart
of reconstructed downtown Beirut. The
five-floor modern building houses his
ateliers, design studio, accessories and
ready-to-wear boutique, couture house
and bridal salon.

In October of the same year, the couturier
showed for the first time his ready-to-
wear collection during Paris Fashion
Week. Suits, cocktail dresses and evening
gowns were paired with handbags, and
a new line of leather goods and accessories
was showcased. This first fashion show
was highly acclaimed by buyers and
enjoyed widespread reviews in the
international media.

In November 2006, the Chambre Syndicale
de la Haute Couture nominated Elie Saab
'Membre Correspondant'. In April 2007, the
couturier confirmed he would make Paris
his second home, by inaugurating a 1000m^2
flagship store in the very heart of the eighth
arrondissement, at 1, Rond-Point des
Champs Elysées. A historical address,
where the finest French couturiers have long
showed their collections, the three-floor
building presented the brand's entire
showcase, including the ready-to-wear
and accessories lines as well as the haute
couture collections in the adjacent salons.

In July 2008, Elie Saab continued to expand
his business internationally by opening
his first UK boutique in London, on the first
floor of the prestigious department store
Harrods, and another one in June 2010,
in Dubai, on the first floor of the luxury circle
of the esteemed Dubai Mall.

In February 2012, Elie Saab opened his
first boutique in Asia, in Hong Kong's
prestigious Landmark Mall in the Central
district. A few months later, in July 2012,
Elie Saab opened his first store in the
Americas: a shop-in-shop at Saks Fifth
Avenue, Santa Fe, in Mexico City, Mexico.
In December of the same year, Elie Saab
opened his first boutique in Switzerland,
on the Quai Général Guisan in Geneva.

4.29

4.28
**Backstage at Elie Saab,
Haute Couture, S/S 2013**
The mixture of lace and
silk give this collection an
elegant finish.

4.29
Silk dress
Silk dress with short sleeves
and lace shoulder inserts.
The skirt has inverted pleats.

Signature

Always on the move, Elie Saab's style is a unique fusion of Western and Eastern cultures, renewing itself with each and every collection. Elie Saab strives for perfection and applies this approach to the whole art of living, an idea inherited from his Lebanese origins. He is particularly fond of modern architecture and design; they are his true passions when he isn't designing.

Elie Saab prefers noble materials such as taffeta, organza, sable and satin paired with more fluid and light fabrics, such as chiffon – for aerial effect – or fine materials like lace. Delicate embroideries made of sequins, semi-precious stones and Swarovski crystals highlight a sublime feminine silhouette.

His perfectionism drives his constant search for the most beautiful fabrics and the finest material, often seeking them out in France and Italy.

The Elie Saab development pillar, the design studio, holds a unique know-how shared by all the sketchers, the embroiderers and the seamstresses. In the same way, the House of Elie Saab works with the most important craft artisans and French and Italian suppliers.

Every year, several hundred dresses are made to order, each one inspected by Elie Saab. In order to reduce the constraints of fittings, regular clients' toiles and bust forms are kept in the atelier. This new form of couture, with irreproachable service, is efficient, ultra competitive and justifies his success.

Elegant details

The wedding dresses designed by Elie Saab contributed to the continued widening of his reputation. So much so that young women from all over the world would travel as far as Paris or Beirut in order to entrust the couturier with the designing of their gowns. Elie Saab has always nursed a true passion for wedding dresses, marvelling at the idea that he is able to make the dreams of young girls into a reality.

Hence why, in July 2003 when the Groupe Pronovias (which specializes in ready-to-wear wedding dresses) suggested to him to create his own line, he accepted without hesitation, glad to be able to offer a less fortunate clientele exceptional wedding dress designs. This licence, established under the name of Elie by Elie Saab, allowed for his wedding dresses to be made available all over the world. This fruitful collaboration marked the beginning of a beautiful story.

In September 2010 Elie Saab launched his own collection of ready-to-wear wedding dresses with 11 new styles, sold exclusively in Paris and Beirut.

4.30
Elie Saab, Haute Couture, S/S 2013
Champagne coloured silk dress on the catwalk.

Toile/muslin/ prototype development

5.1
Christian Lacroix
Christian Lacroix oversees model fittings, selecting fabrics and checking the final fit.

Fit model/mannequin/form

Realizing your designs through the toile development process is very satisfying. There will be mistakes along the way but this is normal and should be expected; nobody ever produces perfect results first time. There will be amendments throughout the process, for example to the details, such as pockets and trims, as well as to the toile fitting itself.

First, choosing the right fabric to sample the toile in is essential. Although calico (woven fabric) is readily available, it won't be any use if you are producing a garment that is meant to be made from a stretch fabric, as you will not get the correct shaping or styling you require. Therefore, try to produce the toile in a fabric closest to the one you intend to make the final garment in. It does not have to be the same, it could be less expensive, but the fabric composition should be similar.

Check your pattern against your working or technical drawing; you will then be able to check that all of the seams are in the correct position, whether they are the correct shape. Are all of the notches in the correct position and have all seam allowances and grainlines, etc. been marked correctly? If there are any discrepancies, it is essential that you check the pattern before cutting it out in fabric.

Try to enjoy this part of the sewing process; it can be frustrating but use it as a time to reflect on your designs. Try to take a flexible approach to this.

In this chapter, there is a guide to moving darts, which is essential for a fitted bodice. The importance of form and silhouette are also discussed. Step-by-step illustrations are provided to guide you through the processes of developing samples, such as fabric manipulation, sewing sleeves, cuffs, collars and pockets. These exercises will help to develop the garment and sample portfolio.

5.2/5.3
Mannequins
These female and male mannequins have detachable limbs, which allow toiles and garments to be fitted with ease. The male half-mannequin is designed for fitting jackets.

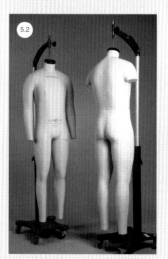
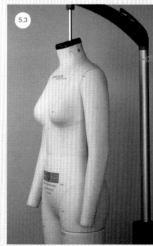

5.4
Fit models
The advantage of fit models is the ability to fit the garment to an actual person; this allows the designer to assess the comfort, fit and overall aesthetic of the garment.

5.5

5.5
Léa Peckre, F/W 2013
White dress with full skirt; this
silhouette is very structured
and defined.

By looking at the overall shape of the
garments in the collection, the designer may
assess form and silhouette. The collection
should represent the ideas and concepts
they wanted to convey. As regards the
silhouette, for example, the garments may
have a particular hemline; the waistlines
may be very shaped or loose. Form is often
determined through the shape and structure
of the garments. For example, when the
garment is modelled, does the fabric convey
movement? A chiffon fabric will flow to
add 'mystery'; heavy cotton may stay static
to add 'control' to the collection. These
elements are important to consider
throughout the entire process, as they will
determine the look of the final collection.

5.6
Dan WJ Prasad, 2013
Experimental tailoring,
capturing both a strong
silhouette and a soft form,
through the use of different
types and weights of fabrics.

5.8

5.8
Bodice toile
A student fits a bodice toile to a mannequin to assess the fit. The toile appears to be tight; therefore, alterations will have to be made to the pattern as well as the toile.

Garment balance, as with form and silhouette, is a crucial element of any collection. Garment balance is the distribution of weight throughout a garment from a central position. This can be assessed when the garment is worn or put on a mannequin. Equal balance gives an overall professional finish to the garment's aesthetic qualities. A correctly balanced garment will feel comfortable when worn. Also, when viewed in the mirror all of the elements such as the hem, shoulder line and neck will fall in the correct position.

To check garment balance, place the garment on a mannequin or a model. For this example, a skirt or dress is used. Stand far enough away so that you can see the entire garment and start at the hem. Does it look straight? If the answer is no and it appears that the garment is falling towards the back or front, the balance needs correcting. There are several other areas to observe: is the shoulder seam, neckline, waist or hem falling to the front or back of the garment? If so, you will have to go back to the pattern and make the amendments. If necessary, another toile will have to be produced to replicate the amendments.

5.7
**Zhang Jingjing, Haute Couture collection,
S/S 2013**
The balance of the dress would have been checked several times before the catwalk show. This hem is informal, rather than straight, but the balance around the hem is evenly distributed so that it is pleasing to the eye.

When making alterations, it is imperative that the designer takes each step at a time. If you try to alter the entire garment, it may result in further problems. For example, if the shoulder seam of a blouse appears to be falling backwards and you recognize that the sleeve is falling forwards, unpick the garment and correct the shoulder seam first, then the sleeve.

5.9
Bodice alterations
The designer is altering the bodice while it is on the mannequin.

5.10
Norman Hartnell, January 1965
Adjustments are made to a stripy jacket backstage at a Norman Hartnell fashion show.

Deconstruction and reconstruction

Deconstruction is a fashion movement that began in the early 1990s; it was a backlash against the brash, ostentatious and materialistic elements of later 1980s and early 90s fashion. This movement resulted in a pared down, simplistic look that has stood the test of time. Designers such as Ann Demeulemeester, Helmut Lang and Martin Margiela were the exponents of such a fashion movement, and their work is still being copied worldwide.

Another form of deconstruction and reconstruction is found within sustainable and ethical fashion, including the process by which clothes are taken apart (deconstruction) and re-sewn (reconstruction) into something new, which is also sometimes known as 'upcycling'. This form of design and construction has gone from exclusive to mainstream, with many retailers now producing such garments to fulfil consumer demands.

5.11

5.11
Junky Styling, multi-lapel dress, 2008
This dress has been recycled from several tailored jackets. They have been deconstructed and sewn back together to produce something new and original.

Developing your own portfolio

Now that you have practised some basic sewing techniques, you can start to develop your own personal portfolio. The techniques range from basic to intermediate and some give you an overview of other techniques, such as dart manipulation. This section will also give you the opportunity to learn how some of the designers featured in the book have constructed elements of their garments. There are in some cases variations of these techniques; however, it is intended that you master the basics first and then start to experiment to develop your own signature, as these designers have done.

When you are completing these exercises in the studio, you will need to have the following:

× Female bodice block
× Shirt pattern
× Various collar patterns.

You will need to compile a sewing equipment list that may consist of the following:

× Lockstitch machine
× Pintuck machine
× Fabric scissors
× Paper scissors
× 3 metres of fabric (preferable calico or medium-weight cotton)
× Tailor's chalk
× Thread
× Hand-sewing needle
× Pins (if necessary)
× Tape measure
× Ruler
× Lockstitch foot
× Invisible zip foot
× Gathering foot
× Pattern paper
× Masking tape
× Lever arch file/pockets or A3 sketchbook (for the portfolio)
× Pen/pencil.

5.12
Comme des Garçons,
S/S 2013
Deconstructed jacket. This design takes the form of irregular shapes that rebel against the uniformity of standard clothing construction and finish.

5.13
Samples
Louise Bennetts' pocket sample.

5.13

5.14

**Pierre Balmain,
S/S 2012**

Knife pleats on this skirt
add a demure look and the
sheer blouse with French
seams finishes the outfit.

Texture

Adding texture to clothing is a unique way of personalizing your designs. Texture can be any surface embellishment, which can be simple or more complex as you have seen in Chapter 4.

The next few pages will take you through several different exercises: pleats, pintucks and tucks. Try to experiment once you have completed them, by using a variety of regular or irregular seam widths. Use heavyweight fabrics and compare the difference between your samples.

Pleats and pintucks

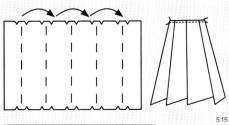

5.15

5.15
Knife pleat
Knife pleat instructions.

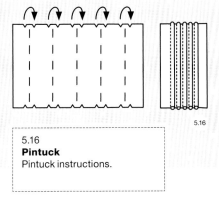

5.16

5.16
Pintuck
Pintuck instructions.

Knife pleats are sharp folds of fabric that lie in the same direction. They can be found in the waists of skirts and trousers.

You will need to use the lockstitch machine and the pintuck machine.

✗ Mark the width of your pleats evenly by measuring along the edge of your calico (for example 4cm (1.57in) apart) and marking each with a notch.

✗ Fold down the centre of each mark, pleat and press each pleat, from the top to the bottom of the fabric.

✗ Sew along the top, 0.5cm (0.19in) from the edge, to secure the pleat.

✗ Press the pleats again, if necessary.

Twin needle pintucks are decorative raised seams.

You will need to use a pintuck machine; it is very similar to the lockstitch, except it has two needles.

✗ Mark the width of your pintucks with a notch, as per the knife pleat, making sure they are parallel to each other (use a smaller width of 2cm (0.78in)). Draw lines from each notch, if it helps to guide you.

✗ Place the needles at either side of the line, with the line/notch directly in the centre.

✗ Sew from the top to the bottom of each line.

Tucks – handstitched

This is a variation of the tucks from Yvonne Lin's interview (Chapter 4). The fabric Yvonne used was very soft, so she has achieved the smooth edges. However, if you are using calico, there will be a variety of different shapes because of the weight of fabric.

You will need a hand-sewing needle and thread.

× Mark rows of dots on a piece of calico approximately 2cm (0.78in) apart.

× Thread the needle; you can put a knot in the end if you wish.

× Sew each row separately, using an up-and-over motion, securing the thread at each end with a knot. Do not pull the thread to ensure that the sample stays flat.

× Then repeat in the opposite direction.

× When complete, pull each thread to gather the swatch and secure each one in place.

× You can press the sample if you wish; this will create a different texture.

5.18

5.18
Yvonne Lin
Tuck sample in bamboo fabric.

5.19
Tucks
Instructions for completing tucks.

5.19

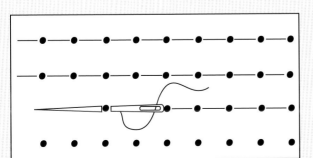
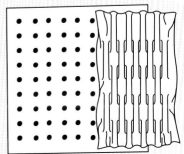

Darts are essential for a garment to fit and accommodate the curves of the body. Darts are particularly important when using woven fabric.

A dart is a stitched fold of fabric that usually tapers to a point. It is a means of suppression, which involves taking fabric out where you don't need it, such as at the shoulder, and letting the fabric out where you do need it, such as over the prominence of the bust.

In Chapter 2, the different types of darts were presented. They can be decorative and used to the designer's advantage; however, knowing how to move darts is important if you want to achieve decorative effects.

This chapter will show you how to move darts using the 'slashing method'. It is a good method to practise before moving on to 'swinging' darts, which is a little more complicated to understand.

Slashing darts

You will need a woman's bodice block, pattern paper, pencil, paper scissors, ruler and masking tape.

Transferring the shoulder dart to the armhole.

× Draw around the bodice block, marking all notches and original dart positions, and cut out.

× Mark the new dart position on the bodice block from its perimeter with a straight line and join this line directly to the bust point.

× Slash along this line to the bust point with scissors.

× Close up the dart that is not required by creasing the dart line from the shoulder to the bust point and folding in the arrowed direction. A dart will now open at the slash line position.

× Place the paper bodice on a clean sheet of paper and trace around, with the new dart clearly marked.

× All manipulation takes place through the bust point.

× In practice, darts are not sewn directly to the bust point, as this would look very unflattering; the dart will end 1.5 to 2cm (0.59 to 0.78in) away from the bust point.

Duro Olowu, S/S 2009
Cleverly positioned waist darts
give this outfit a sleek,
sophisticated silhouette.

5.21
1
Paper bodice block with
new dart position marked (A).

2
New dart position has been
slashed (cut) (A), closed at
the neck dart (B) and original
waist dart (C).

3
Bodice block showing new
dart positions.

5.21

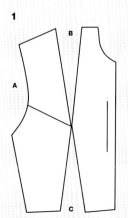

1

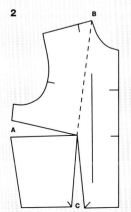

2

3

Sleeves are designed in various shapes, styles and widths; some of the different types are:

Set-in sleeve

A standard sleeve that you will find in shirts. They are very basic, do not have many details and are functional rather than decorative.

Two-piece sleeve

Some tailored jackets have two-piece sleeves. They are designed to mimic the shape and movement of the arm. They consist of two pieces that, when sewn together, produce a curve at the elbow.

Raglan sleeve

The sleevehead (top of the sleeve) starts at the neck point. It is normally sewn to the bodice, as opposed to a set-in sleeve, which is sewn into the armhole. This type of sleeve can be found on sweatshirts and sportswear.

Kimono sleeve

This style originates from the Japanese kimono and is still very popular today. This type of sleeve is not joined together at the bodice. The bodice and sleeve are cut and sewn as one piece.

5.22
Kate Waterhouse wears dress by Gucci at Mercedes Benz Fashion Week, S/S 2013/14
Dress with lantern-style sleeve, which is fitted at the bicep and cuff, with added volume in-between.

5.23
Set-in sleeve
Diagram for sewing a
set-in sleeve.

5.23

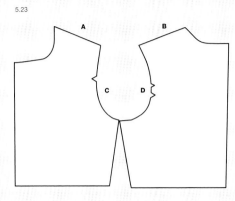

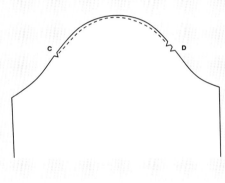

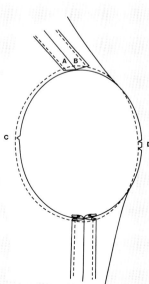

Set-in sleeve

This exercise will help you put the components of a shirt together, starting with the set-in sleeve. Funmilayo Deri (Chapter 4) used this sleeve in several of her dresses.

You will need a shirt pattern, front and back bodice and sleeve only, and a gathering foot.

x Cut out the front and back bodices and sleeve.

x Sew the shoulder seams together using 1cm (0.39in) seam allowance. Press the seam open (A and B).

x Sew the side seams together with a 1cm (0.39in) seam allowance. Press the seam open.

x Change the foot on the lockstitch machine to a gathering foot.

x Place the sleeve on the lockstitch machine. Between the front and back notches (C and D), gather the sleeve head 0.5cm (0.19in) from the edge. Gathering the sleeve head will allow you to sew in the sleeve easily.

x Replace the gathering foot with the lockstitch foot.

x Match the notches on the sleeve to the front and back notches on the bodice (A and B, C and D). You can use pins but do not sew over them as they will break your needle. If it helps, hand-stitch the sleeve into the armhole.

x With a 1cm (0.39in) seam allowance, start sewing from the underarm point, making sure the notches match as you sew around.

x When you have finished, you should not have gathers in the sleeve head, it should be slightly raised, and this is to allow for comfort when the garment is worn.

x Press the sleeve.

'Design is
a constant
challenge
to balance
comfort
with luxe,
the practical
with the
desirable.'

Donna Karan

5.24
Funmilayo Deri
Silk hooded jacket with
set-in sleeve (sewn as
per instructions).

5.25
Emma Hardstaff
Pleated denim cocoon coat.

Collars

Collars are neckline finishes that vary in style, shape and size. They can be produced in a variety of fabrics. Some of the different types are:

Shirt collar

There are variations of shirt collars: some are designed with a separate stand, others are not. The stand is the piece of fabric that sits next to the neck. The collar is the extended section that falls over the collar stand.

Mandarin

This is the 'stand' of the shirt only, it can vary in style and width.

Peter Pan

A curved collar that sits next to the bodice and is not raised up with a stand.

Tailored collar

A tailored collar consists of a collar and revers. The revers is cut as part of the bodice and is the lower section of the collar. The collar is a separate piece that is sewn to the back neck and revers. It is also known as a notched collar.

5.26
Funmilayo Deri, A/W 2012
Luxurious velvet, high-collar dress with draped bodice.

5.26

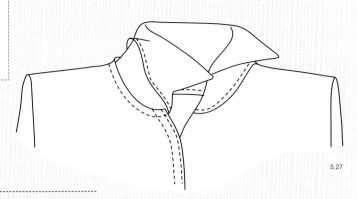

5.27

Shirt collar

A standard men's shirt collar is made of four pieces of fabric: two for the collar and two for the collar stand. Most shirts, particularly men's business shirts, are interfaced to maintain firmness. Sewing a collar is not difficult but you will need to be accurate. Areas to be aware of are the collar points (these are the pointed ends of the collar); this is where you will need to refer to the 'Needle Control' section (see pages 56-57). You always sew the collar section first, then snip the corners and turn it through to right side and press. The collar is then sandwiched between the collar stands.

Some shirt collars can be cut in one piece without a seam. The following exercise is based on this type of collar; then, once you have mastered this, try a separate collar with stand. Again, extra care must be taken when sewing; you will need to be accurate to ensure that the collar is sewn the same at either side.

You will need a men's shirt collar pattern and interfacing.

✕ Cut pieces out of calico and attach interfacing to one piece only.

✕ With the interfaced collar, turn up and press a seam of 1cm (0.39in) at the neck edge. Topstitch this seam approximately 0.7cm (0.27in) in from the edge.

✕ Place the upper and lower collars together on the right side. When you match the top of the collars together, you will see that the top collar is 1cm (0.39in) longer, which is correct.

✕ Sew around the edge of the collar with a seam allowance of 1cm (0.39in).

✕ Trim the sewn seam down to 0.5cm (0.19in). Turn through to the right side and press it flat.

✕ Join the raw edge of the collar to the right outside of the neck edge. Sew a seam of 1cm (0.39in). Press seam open.

✕ With the topstitched edge of the collar, place this on the inside (wrong side) of the neck edge.

✕ Edge-stitch the seam approximately 0.2cm (0.08in) from the edge.

✕ Press collar.

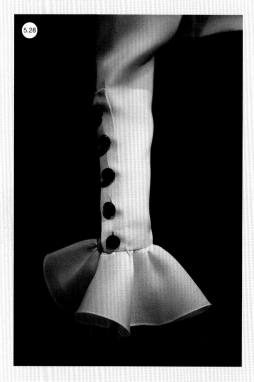

5.28

Cuffs

Most shirts have a standard cuff. Cuffs can be rounded off at the edges or square. The double cuff has an extension that turns back and is secured with a cuff link; it is also known as a French cuff. A frilled cuff is a flamboyant and decorative cuff.

This exercise is for sewing a basic cuff with a placket opening. Also known as a gauntlet opening, this is the extra piece of fabric attached to the opening of the cuff that accommodates the buttons and buttonholes.

Cuff with gauntlet

There are various finishes for shirt cuffs such as a placket (see example), a finished opening (normally bound) or elasticated. The majority of men's long-sleeve shirts have a placket.

There are several ways in which to learn how to sew a placket; one option is to take an old shirt and unpick the cuff and placket, making a note of each stage as you unpick it. This will form the basis of your instruction when sewing it back up. In addition, look at the type of interlining and where it is positioned.

5.28
Nan Kempner, 'Une Americaine A Paris', 1964
White silk sleeve with buttoned cuff and frill. This cuff is similar to the cuff with gauntlet, except an extension has been added in place of the gauntlet.

5.29
Cuff placket with gauntlet insertion
Diagram for cuff placket construction (see page 145).

5.29

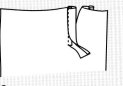
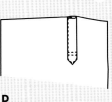

A   B   C   D

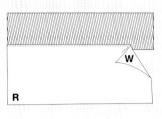

5.30
Diagram of cuff construction
The placket is always sewn on before the cuff.

R = right side
W = wrong side

Gauntlet insertion

You will need: cuff pattern, gauntlet template, shirt sleeve pattern and interfacing.

A

Cut out the cuff, gauntlet and sleeve. Place the interlinging and one piece of the cuff on a fusing press to bond them together.

B

With the right side of the gauntlet facing the wrong side of the sleeve, position the gauntlet so that it is level with the edge of the sleeve and directly over the opening. With a seam allowance of 0.6cm (0.23in), sew the gauntlet along each side of the opening.

C

Turn the sleeve over to the right side and fold the shorter side over, enclosing the raw edge. Fold the edge over, place just over the first stitch line and topstitch as close to the edge as possible.

D

Fold the longer side of the gauntlet through the right side. If it does not fold over easily, snip diagonally into the corner to release fabric. Finally, in one motion sew following the shape of the gauntlet. Press flat.

5.30

Cuff

× Fold the edge of the interfaced cuff up by 1cm (0.39in), press flat and topstitch approximately 0.7cm (0.27in) from the edge.

× Place the right sides of the cuffs together (raw edges) and sew them using a 1cm (0.39in) seam allowance. Trim the seam down to 0.5cm (0.19in).

× With the gathering foot, gather the sleeve hem, then measure and ensure that the cuff is the same width.

× With the right sides together, place the raw edge of the cuff to the bottom of the sleeve, starting at the opening of the gauntlet. With a seam of 1cm (0.39in) sew around the cuff.

× Place the interfaced side down and edge stitch 0.2cm (0.08in) from the edge.

Collar variations

The next few exercises will help you with 'needle control'. They include a Mandarin collar, Peter Pan collar and a tailored collar.

Mandarin collar

This Mandarin collar has piping inserted into the collar edge but you could use any decorative trim, such as lace.

You will need: Mandarin shirt collar pattern, shirt pattern (front and back), front and back facing patterns, interlining, binding, piping, invisible zip foot and lockstitch foot.

✕ Cut out all of your pieces. Interface the front and back facings and the top collar only.

✕ Cut the piping so that it is at least 3cm (1.18in) longer than the collar length, then insert into the binding. Using an invisible zip foot (this allows you to get close to the binding edge), sew this section (A).

✕ Change to the lockstitch foot. With a seam of 0.5cm (0.19in) sew the piping to one side of the collar only, with the raw edges together (B).

✕ Take the top collar and place right sides together (the piping will be sandwiched between the two layers) (B). With a 0.5cm (0.19in) seam allowance, sew the collar edges and piping together. With a pair of scissors snip around the collar edge, then turn it through to the right side and press.

✕ Sew the front and back bodice shoulder seams together and press open.

✕ Matching the centre back points and the collar notches (right sides together), sew a seam of 0.6cm (0.23in). Place the facing on the front, so that the collar is sandwiched between the front bodice and the facing and sew along the edge with a 1cm (0.39in) seam. Snip along the curve. Edge stitch along the facing side only (as close to the seam as possible). Turn through to the right side and press (C).

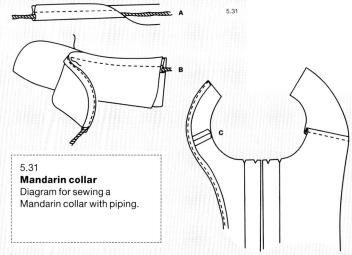

5.31

5.31
Mandarin collar
Diagram for sewing a
Mandarin collar with piping.

146

Peter Pan collar

Peter Pan collars are starting to gain more popularity. Once the choice for little girls' dresses, in recent years they have become more mainstream within womenswear and menswear.

You will need: Peter Pan collar pattern, shirt pattern, binding, piping, invisible zip foot, lockstitch foot and interfacing.

✕ Cut out all of your pieces and interface one collar.

✕ Cut the piping so that it is at least 3cm (1.18in) longer than the collar length (A), then insert into the binding. Using an invisible zip foot (this allows you to get close to the binding edge), sew this section.

✕ Change to the lockstitch foot. With a seam of 0.5cm (0.19in) sew the piping to one side of the collar only, with the raw edges together (B).

✕ Take the top collar and place with the right sides together (the piping will be sandwiched between the two layers). With a 1cm (0.39in) seam allowance, sew the collar edges and piping together. With a pair of scissors snip around the collar edge, then turn it through to the right side and press (C and D).

✕ Matching the centre back points and the collar, sew a seam of 1cm (0.39in). Ensure that you pivot this around so that the edges meet as you are sewing.

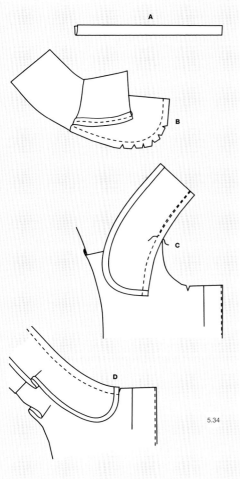

A

B

C

D

5.34

5.35
Collar and revers
Wool coat with traditional collar and revers, circa 1960s.

5.36
Collar construction
Diagram showing how to construct the collar.

Tailored jacket collar

This collar is also known as a collar and revers or notched collar. It can be found on men's and women's tailored jackets and coats.

You will need: tailored jacket pattern (front and back), collar, lockstitch foot, interfacing.

× Cut out all the pieces and interface one collar.

× To make the collar, place the right sides together and, with a seam allowance of 1cm (0.39in), stitch around the edge. Trim the seam down to 0.5cm (0.19in). Turn through and press. Topstitch along the outer edge (two rows in the example, but one is fine) (A).

× With the right sides together, sew the underside of the collar (the piece that has not been interfaced to the neck), starting at the centre back. Remember, you are not sewing all of the layers together, only the bottom one (B).

× Ensure that you pivot the collar so that the notches match up with the shoulder seam (C).

× Sew all the layers of the fabric together, ensuring that they are positioned correctly.

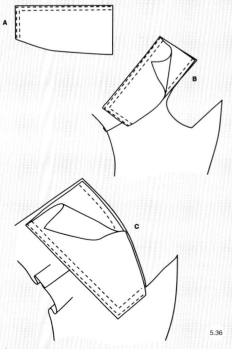

A

B

C

5.36

5.37
Gucci, F/W 2013
Men's double-breasted coat with contrasting fur collar and revers.

Pockets can be both decorative and functional. In either case, it is important to consider size, placement and types of finish. They can be finished in self-fabric or contrast fabric (as a design feature).

Some different styles of pocket are as follows:

Patch pockets

Round, square, or any shape for that matter, patch pockets are one of the easiest to create. They are placed flat on top of the garment and stitched around the edge, leaving an opening at the top. They can be made with or without a lining, and are mainly seen on shirts and jackets.

Patch pocket with flap

As per the patch pocket but with an extra flap that hangs over the pocket opening.

5.38
Welted pockets
Welted pockets on a traditional waistcoat and jacket.

Trouser/jeans pockets

These have either a curved pocket opening or a strain opening that can be cut at an angle.

Jetted pocket

Often found on men's tailored trousers and jackets. The opening is two strips of fabric, and on the inside of the garment there is a pocket bag sewn to these two strips.

In-seam pocket

These pockets are inserted into the seam of the garment and a zip or buttons are used to close them.

Welt/breast pocket

Found on the breast of men's jackets and set into the jacket.

Welt pocket

You will need: welt pocket pattern pieces, lockstitch foot, interfacing, tailor's chalk, an extra piece of calico (approximately 30x30cm (11.8x11.8in)) to sew the pocket on to.

✕ Cut out all of the pattern pieces and fuse half of the welt piece.

✕ With tailor's chalk, mark on the right side of the calico the position of the pocket (this measurement should be taken from the welt minus the seam allowance).

✕ Fold the welt lengthwise with the right sides together and sew along each end where the notches are marked. Trim the edges, turn through and press.

✕ Place the welt on to the large pocket bag. All of the raw edges should be level and it should be placed centrally so that there is an equal gap at both sides. Sew along the top 0.6cm (0.23in) from the edge.

✕ Place the welt face down along the marked position of the pocket opening. Sew from one end of the welt to the other, not from the edge of the pocket back. Secure at either end with a reverse stitch.

✕ Lift the top of the pocket bag and welt down and mark a point 0.6cm (0.23in) from each end of the line. Carefully cut diagonally towards the stitch line at the top of the welt, not the pocket bag. Do this at both ends.

✕ Place the smaller pocket bag on top of the larger one and sew along the upper edge of the pocket opening.

✕ Turn the entire pocket through to the right side. Press the welt upwards and into position and edge stitch at either side, approximately 0.3cm (0.12in) from the edge (A).

✕ Turn the pocket over to the right side and sew the pocket bags together (B).

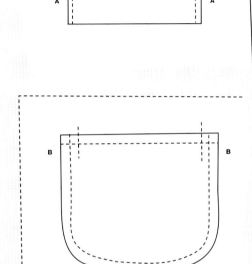

5.39

Victoria Whittaker graduated from Manchester Metropolitan University in 2013 with a BSc (Hons) in Clothing Design and Technology. She has been nominated for the Drapers Technical Textiles Award 2013.

Project inspiration

Victoria visited a music festival in the summer of 2012 and at the end she noticed that hundreds of tents had been left behind by people who could not be bothered to take them home. Volunteers were driving over the tents in little buggies (carts) to flatten them, then collecting them and dumping them in a pile. She wondered at the time what was going to happen to them, and thought it was such a waste. Victoria then decided to do some research into festival tents, which inspired her to begin the perfect upcycling research project.

Design inspiration

The fashion trend that inspired the design of the jacket came from Promostyle Summer 2014, called 'Marine' and it relates to the sea. This theme has been expanded with extra research into RNLI lifeboats and the beach, which influenced the style lines and surface design of the jacket.

There are several design features that cross over between the three influences of the tent, the RNLI and the beach. These features were demonstrated on the research board and are reflected in the construction details of the final jacket.

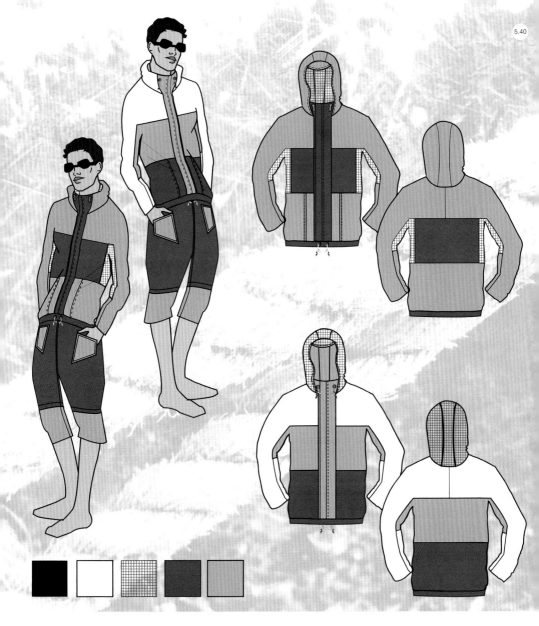

5.40
Development and inspiration board for Victoria's jacket
The design maintains the RNLI influence and the techniques used to develop the texture.

Construction

The tent was used at 'V' fest in 2012 and was upcycled into the reversible jacket.

The brass ringlet holes used on the hood and the hem of the jacket for the draw cord to pass through are rings used for securing the ground sheet of the tent.

The yellow and grey fabric used in the jacket were both taken from the outer tent.

The black net fabric used in the underarm panels of the jacket and inside the hood is taken from the inner tent door, and would be used in the tent as a fly barrier. This net was chosen for the underarm panels to help moisture to be released from the wearer to the outside to help keep them cool.

On the reverse side of the jacket, the roof of the inner tent was stitched over the top of the back panels.

The two pocket panels at the bottom of the yellow side of jacket were taken from the outer tent windows.

The draw cords used in the hood and the hem of the jacket were originally used as the guide ropes of the tent.

The zip fastening was taken from the outer tent door opening. The tent door has a zip toggle on both sides so it can be unzipped from both outside and inside the tent; this worked perfectly as a reversible zip on the jacket.

The white fabric in the jacket was taken from the inner tent. It is the only fabric used in the jacket which is not water resistant so it was used on the reverse side of the jacket.

5.41

Component parts

The images show the tent and the areas the designer identified as component parts for the jacket. This maintains the overall theme and utilizes responsible recycling processes.

Process

The main priority areas that had to be considered when developing patterns for the jacket were comfort, aesthetics and functionality:

× Displacing the shoulder seams of the jacket to avoid water getting in.

× Developing a gusset to enable 'lift' and 'reach' in the sleeve.

× Developing a drawstring hood with a peak.

× Developing a zip opening and stand that work the same when reversed.

× Making the jacket reversible and fully functional on both sides.

× Incorporating an eco-friendly handicraft method to the jacket.

Sewing techniques

Victoria decided that it was important that the entire jacket was created entirely from materials and items taken from the two-man tent; no other materials taken from elsewhere were to be used.

The zip fastening was taken from the outer tent door opening. The tent door has a zip toggle on both sides so it could be unzipped from both outside and inside the tent, which worked perfectly as a reversible zip on the jacket. Victoria encountered a problem with the tent zip as it was not open ended; this affected the design because although the jacket could be unzipped, it could not be fully opened at the hem and therefore had to be pulled on over the head.

The draw cords used in the hood and the hem of the jacket were originally used as the guide ropes of the tent.

The two fake pocket panels at the bottom of the yellow side of the jacket were taken from the outer tent windows.

The yellow and grey fabrics were both taken from the outer tent. The white fabric was taken from the inner tent; it was the only fabric used that was not water resistant and was therefore used on the reverse side of the jacket.

Victoria utilized as much of the tent as she could. The back net fabric used in the underarm panels and inside the hood was taken from the inner tent door, and would normally be used in the tent as a fly barrier. This net was chosen for the underarm panels to help moisture release and keep the wearer cool.

On the reverse side of the jacket, the roof of the inner tent was stitched over the top of the back panels.

The tent fabric, being 100% polyester, has thermoplastic properties: it can be moulded into a shape and heated then, once cooled, permanently retains that shape. Texture for the jacket was created with shell fragments found at Mundesley beach, which were tied tightly into the grey tent fabric with polyester thread. This fabric was then steamed in a vegetable steamer for 45 minutes. Once the shells were removed from the fabric, the surface was patterned in a raised shell-like relief. These panels were sewn into the front of the jacket.

Born in Paris in 1984, Léa Peckre grew up in an artistic environment where the cinema and photography both had a major role.

Soon attracted by artistic studies, Léa discovered and developed an interest in construction and design through the practice of ceramics and textiles. Her art academic studies were followed by a specialization in fashion design, which led her to study at the prestigious fashion and design school La Cambre in Brussels in 2004.

In 2011, after graduating with high distinction, Léa Peckre won the L'Oreal Professional Jury Grand Prize at the 25th International Hyères Festival with the collection 'Cemeteries are Fields of Flowers'. During her scholarship, she also won other prestigious prizes: La Cambre Award (2010), Rue Blanche Award (2010) and City of Paris Fashion Award (2008).

After starting her career at famous fashion houses, such as Jean Paul Gaultier, Givenchy and Isabel Marant, Léa Peckre launched her own brand with a Spring/Summer 2013 collection entitled 'A Light in the Dark'.

Where do you get your inspiration?

I'm mostly inspired by architecture and light, I feel close to the Romantic painters' view, like Caspar David Friedrich. But to be honest, I can be inspired by anything.

Do you believe the creative process involves all aspects of garment realization?

In my creative process, every idea is linked to fabrics, to 3D. During the entire process, I work on completion models, joining models, experiments on fabrics, pattern drafting.

When do you consider the types of sewing techniques you intend to use within your collections?

As soon as I develop the fabrics, I think about the sewing techniques I will have to use. I gradually do some tests, samples and I can't stop until I've found the perfect completion. When I visualize the final collection, I have to make sure there is coherence between all garments, considering the sewing techniques.

5.42
Textured skirt
Organic forms brings definition to this textured skirt, which is streamlined with a fitted, cropped jumper.

How much time do you spend considering sewing techniques within the creative process?

Considering the sewing techniques is a significant part of the creative process, because it provides neatness to the garment.

When visualizing the finished collection, do you think trims/notions are an important feature?

I am fond of notions. For example, in my latest collection, I used rib trimming and zip fasteners. These ones are visible, so everything has to be meticulously finished and has to match perfectly with the garment's proportions.

5.43
Sheer skirt
The waist detail is emphasized by the print, which is cleverly constructed in tulip folds on this sheer skirt.

5.44
Sculptured top
Fitted, sculptured woolen top is worn with layered, textured and sheer skirt.

How important is sewing within the garment realization process?

Sewing needs a perfect knowledge of the garment, precision, fastidiousness and perfectionism, that's why it requires time and professionalism.

What types of fabrics do you like to use?

I like crêpe, silk, woollen fabrics and some high-end lingerie fabrics.

What advice would you give to new designers?

Being passionate, self-demanding and not frightened by work.

5.45
Dress
High-waisted, two-tone dress with textured cummerbund.

5.46
Jacket and trousers
A striking silhouette with a waist-defining jacket and wide leg trousers.

6

Innovation
within industry

6.1
Iris Van Herpen, 2011
Three-dimensional dress.

Innovation within the fashion and clothing industry can be anything from computer-generated 3D garment design to upcycling of clothing. Innovation offers designers a creative outlet in which to experiment with new ideas in areas such as sportswear design, which then becomes mainstream and filters through to the high street.

The use of CAD (computer-aided design) or CAM (computer-aided manufacture), saves retailers money, particularly in the pre-production process, as they do not have to commit to materials and extra resources. CAD enables the designer or retailer to visualize a collection and buying decisions can be made based on this prior to making financial commitments.

There are constantly new, emerging technologies in fashion design and construction. A few to mention are 'see before you sew' technologies, which come in the form of 3D garment modelling, whereby the designer can produce his or her own avatar. These avatars can be given the same personal measurements as a model. During this process 2D patterns are applied to the model to produce a fully formed garment. This process also allows the designer to assess the fit of the garment or even to see what a product range or collection would look like.

Three-dimensional body scanners are another recent innovation within fashion, often used within the lingerie industry, where fit is paramount. These systems enable hundreds of body measurements to be taken, so that the garment can be personally fitted to a customer.

6.2

Three-dimensional printers are excellent tools for producing prototypes, particularly within sportswear. These printers produce a 'flat pattern' on specially formulated paper, which can then be made into a prototype product. The prototype is normally finished in the chosen design and again allows the retailer or designer to view, assess and analyse the commercial viability of the product. Technology in the fashion industry is essential; excellent tools help to aid creativity.

6.2
Gareth Pugh
Dress made with silvered leather. Displayed at the 'Ballgowns: British Glamour Since 1950' exhibition at the Victoria and Albert Museum in 2012.

6.3
Hussein Chalayan, 'Readings', 2009.
This collection includes crystals and LED flickering lights.

Technology-driven construction techniques have been informed by traditional sewing techniques. The need to develop more sophisticated construction techniques is often a response to the new fabric developments that offer enhanced qualities, such as keeping the wearer warm or cool. Here, traditional sewing techniques may not be suitable as they do not mirror the fabric structure or qualities.

Consider, for example, the construction of wetsuits. The first process is 'adhesive bonding', whereby glue is applied to the seams to prevent water from entering the seam. The second process is to sew the seam, which allows for more movement in the body during wear.

Thermal bonding is a non-sew construction process that requires thermo-plastic polymers in the materials used. When the heat is applied during the process, this bonds the seams together. This construction technique requires no needle, thread or glue.

There are countless other technological advances in sewing techniques that are developing all the time. However, on a day-to-day basis, millions of garments are produced using traditional sewing techniques, without which the technology would not exist.

6.5

6.5
**Iris Van Herpen,
Voltage, 2013**
Environmental interaction with the human body is the theme of this 3D printed dress.

6.4
Pierre Cardin, F/W 1959
Model in coat with moulded collar.

Is 3D printing in the fashion industry a good thing?

To examine whether or not 3D printing is a useful tool in the fashion industry, we need to look at how it could be used. This could include the following three areas:

× Instant disposable fashion

× High-end couture garments

× High-tech, form-fitting sportswear.

In all instances, the bottom line is 'can a profit be made?'

6.6
Engineered Distortion, designed by Amelia Agosta, 2012, L'Oreal Melbourne Fashion Festival: The National Graduate showcase
Body scanning and 3D printing were used to design Amelia's collection.

Instant disposable fashion

Just as shopping online has become part of our everyday existence, one can envisage 3D printing technology being used by low-price fashion clothing retailers to offer customers a high-end 'bespoke' finish to their clothing; in essence, using products already designed for standard body sizes and tailoring them to a customer's specific shape. The cost argument could be softened by the knowledge that in order to pay for the initial outlay of 3D technology the retailer could levy a charge for the service, which may in the long run lead to an increase in profits.

6.6

High-end couture garments

Some people within the fashion industry have stated that designer or couture clothing looks best on thinner models, whilst trying to sell their designs to the masses. By investing in 3D printing technology fashion designers could customize their designs to suit all body shapes, whether by repositioning a particular 3D print to guide the eye away from perceived imperfections or creating an illusion similar to a 'trompe l'oeil' to an observer.

6.7
Hussein Chalayan
Tulle dress from the *British Design 1948–2012: Innovation in the Modern Age* exhibition at the V&A, 2012.

6.7

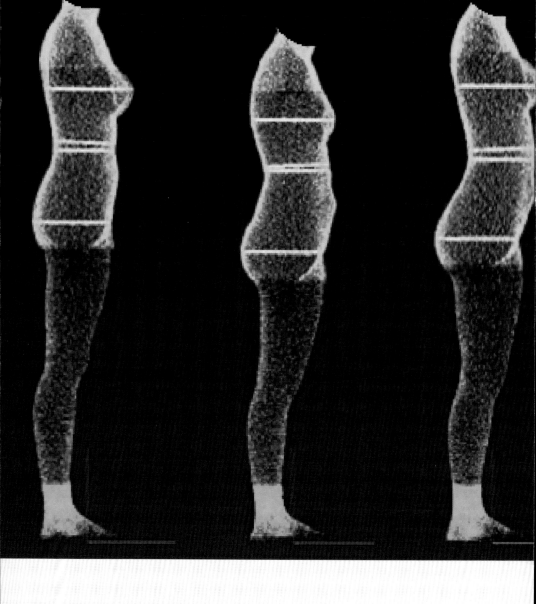

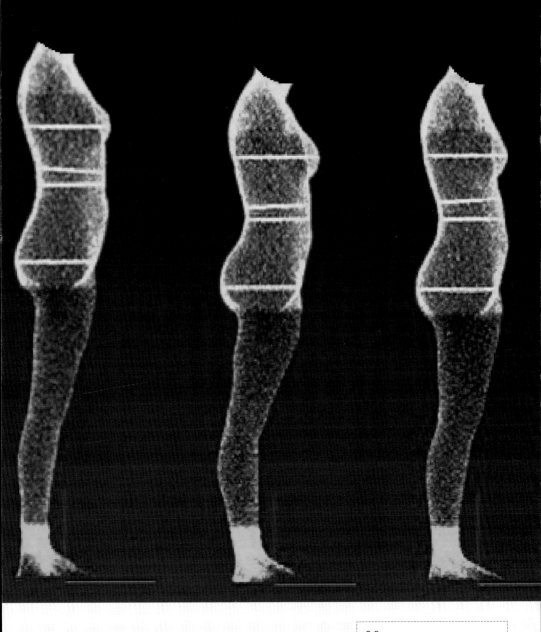

6.8
3D body scanner
Hundreds of measurements are recorded with this equipment to build up an accurate 3D representation of an individual figure.

High-tech form-fitting sportswear

The 2012 Olympics and Paralympics could
be used to illustrate that sportswear would
greatly benefit from 3D printing technology:
within sport, there is no 'standard size'
for a competitor. With the introduction
of 3D technology in the design process,
a body-scanner similar to current airline
security systems could be used to gather
and store accurate measurements and
data for an individual athlete. Fabrics could
be tested for myriad athletic conditions,
ensuring that the initial fit and final
construction results in an effective garment.

6.9
**Speedo Fastskin FSII
swimsuit**
This swimsuit was designed
to improve swimming
performance. Body scanning
equipment was used to
develop the close fit, and
fabrics were developed along
with construction techniques
so the athlete could
concentrate on technique
without compromising comfort.

Body scanning

3D body scanners are used in sportswear to make customized garments for the wearer. However, they are becoming increasingly popular in mainstream fashion. They can be used in the production of undergarments, whereby a better fit would be achieved rather than using standardized measurements. The 3D body scanner takes hundreds of measurements, including the unique ability to take circumference measurements. It then produces an outline of the body with details of all of the measurements taken. This technology holds great potential for the fashion industry, not only in the made-to-measure sector but also in terms of sustainability. The use of 3D printers to produce the garment immediately for sale to the customer also has the potential to reduce waste.

6.10
Nike Pro Turbo tracksuit
This tracksuit features drag-resistant insertions to improve speed when running.

Conclusion

Sewing Techniques aims to provide you with a basic understanding of how the process of sewing influences the design process. Sewing is often seen as the last stage in any project but it is hoped that through this book, you can see that creativity is a combination of all things. Sewing can be used at the research stage to develop concepts. In some cases it can replace the traditional process of sketching by photographing images and translating what you see through the use of sewing techniques.

This book also aims to inspire those new to sewing and to encourage them to experiment with techniques. This will lead to a greater understanding of what can be applied effectively to enhance your designs. For the more experienced, it provides an additional element to the design process. Many designers are now trying to achieve a much more individual and exclusive handwriting to their collections, making them instantly recognizable by fashion industry professionals.

The future of garment construction is dependent upon a basic understanding of sewing techniques and this book provides a snapshot of some of those techniques. It is hoped that you will find inspiration to pursue your career in this most creative of industries. As the interviews and case studies in these pages demonstrate, it is also most rewarding.

Many sewing tools and the corresponding terminology have not changed for hundreds of years; for example, the 18th-century tool known as an awl (used for piercing holes in fabric or paper to mark the position of a dart) is still used today. Of course, depending on where you live in the world, different terminology means the same thing. For example in Europe, a mannequin is the same as the US dress stand. However, as the fashion industry operates on an international level, it is important to understand the different terms in order to aid communication within the fashion supply chain.

Terminology

Bar tack
Stitches used to reinforce edges, such as on a belt loop.

Bias
45-degree angle from the straight of the grain.

Block
A standard size basic pattern, which is used to make garments.

Bobbin/spool
A piece of equipment used to wind thread. Once this procedure is complete, the bobbin is inserted into the bobbin case. The bobbin thread forms the bottom thread of the stitch formation.

Bobbin/spool case
The case in which the bobbin is inserted.

Bodice
The top part of the dress, from shoulder to upper hip.

Croquis
A quick drawing or sketch.

Darts
A stitched fold of fabric, which usually tapers to a point. A dart is a means of suppression, which involves taking out fabric where you do not need it. They help to shape the garment, for example at the bust point, and can be decorative.

Fabric composition
What the fabric is made up of, for example, 90% cotton, 10% polyester.

Facing
A shaped piece of fabric sewn to the raw edge of the garment and folded inside. This is normally interfaced to make the section stable. This type of facing can be found on the inside of the neck, known as a neck facing. There are also other types of facings, such as jacket facings, which are constructed using a different method.

Fuse
This is the process whereby the adhesive side of the interlining is attached to the fabric using heat.

Gathering foot
An attachment that adds fullness by gathering the fabric as it stitches.

Gathers
A long piece of fabric that is gathered using a specialist machine foot or wide sewing stitch to add fullness to a garment. Gathers can be found in areas such as the sleevehead or waist.

Grain or grainline
Direction of the fabric that runs parallel to the selvedge.

Grown-on
This is a collar and collar stand that are cut in one piece rather than two seperate pieces; used for example on a traditional dress shirt.

Interfacing
A material coated with an adhesive side on one side that is heat-sealed to the fabric to provide stability to certain areas of a garment, such as waistbands and collars.

Lining
Fabric used to conceal the inside of a garment, such as a jacket. It is normally a lightweight fabric, specifically produced for this purpose.

Lower thread tension screw
This is the small screw located on the side of the bobbin/spool case next to the thread slot.

Nap/pile
Found in fabrics such as velvet or corduroy. These have raised fibres, which produce a shaded effect to the fabric when smoothed by hand in a certain direction. Extra care should be taken to ensure that all pattern pieces are cut out in the same direction.

Needle
Universal needles are suitable for woven fabrics, ballpoint needles for sewing jersey fabrics and there are a variety of other needles for specialist fabrics such as leather and stretch fabrics.

Notches
Marks on patterns used to match seams. They are also used to indicate darts, pleats and so on. These may come in the form of a short line on an industrial pattern or a diamond shape on a commercial pattern.

Notions/trims
Haberdashery, such as buttons, zips and decorative trims.

Overlocker/serger
Machine used to conceal the raw edges of the fabric to prevent the fraying of a seam.

Pleats
Folded sections of fabric, which can be used in place of darts or gathering at the waist of a skirt. There are several different types of pleat, such as inverted and knife.

Revers
This is the front part of the jacket that is folded back on the chest and the collar is sewn to this section.

Scye
Armhole of a garment.

Seam
The sewn join between two pieces of fabric; the width varies according to the type of seam.

Seam allowances
The seam allowance is the space between the edge of the fabric and the stitch line; this measurement will vary depending on the type of seam required for production.

Selvedge
The edges of the fabric that prevent the fibres unravelling. A woven number or manufacturer's name or style number may be printed or woven along this edge.

Stitch length
Stitch length can be varied according to the type of stitch you require to complete your task.

Stretch fabric
A fabric either produced from natural or synthetic fibres that has a four-way stretch (stretchable in four directions). For example, the fabric used to produce stretchable sportswear garments.

Tension discs
Two metal discs on the front of the industrial sewing machine with a tension dial; the top thread is looped through these.

Walking foot
Also known as a 'dual feed foot', used for sewing several layers of fabric together to prevent them from slipping whilst sewing; this would be suitable for silk fabrics, for example.

Woven fabric
A fabric which has been woven and can only be stretched on the bias, such as cotton.

Zip or zipper
A fastening that is used on various garments, such as skirts, trousers and jackets. Consists of a zip pull and zip teeth.

Coolhunting
www.coolhunting.com
Cool Hunting features stories and videos highlighting creativity and innovation in design, technology, style, culture, food and travel. With a global team of editors and contributors it consists of daily updates and weekly mini-documentaries.

Fashion and Textile Museum, London
www.ftmlondon.org
Contemporary fashion design from clothing to accessories. Includes some of Britain's iconic designers, such as Mary Quant and Vivienne Westwood.

Inhabitat
www.inhabitat.com
Inhabitat.com is a weblog devoted to the future of design, tracking the innovations in technology, practices and materials that are pushing architecture and home design towards a smarter and more sustainable future.

Lookbook.nu
www.lookbook.nu
This blogging site brings together creative, passionate and open-minded fashion enthusiasts, and democratically recognizes the talents of real people from around the world.

Modeconnect.com
www.modeconnect.com
This site provides resources for all those interested in creating fashion. It offers a worldwide platform on which fashion students, educators and young designers can show their work and share information. Recently Modeconnect has launched a feature dedicated to young designers at different stages in their training.

Musée Galliera, Paris
www.paris.fr
Housed in a 19th-century palace owned by the Duchess Galliera, the capital of fashion's most exceptional museum preserves a staggering 70,000 articles of clothing. Naturally, France's historical fashion icons Marie-Antoinette and Empress Josephine are represented heavily in the collection, with contemporary pieces from the likes of Jean Paul Gaultier and Yves Saint Laurent.

PYMCA
www.pymca.com
PYMCA is a highly specialized archive, sourcing and representing images of international youth culture and social history. The archive spans over a century, celebrating people's self-expression, energy and after passion featuring images of fashion, music, art, design, etc. This is a good resource for referencing different types of clothing.

Selvedge
www.selvedge.org
Selvedge magazine can be purchased both online and in hardcopy. This resource brings together world's finest textile photography, unparalleled design and peerless writing. Directed towards an international, discerning audience, Selvedge covers fine textiles in every context: fine art, interiors, fashion, travel and shopping. It is published every other month.

The Business of Fashion (bof)
www.flipboard.com
Up to the minute articles from the fashion industry, which also includes new and emerging contemporary designers.

The Fashion Museum
www.museumofcostume.co.uk
The Fashion Museum is one of the world's great museum collections of historic and fashionable dress. Designated as a collection of outstanding national significance, the Fashion Museum was recently listed by CNN as one of the world's Top 10 fashion museums.

The Metropolitan Museum of Art
www.metmuseum.org
The Metropolitan Museum of Art was founded on 13 April, 1870, "to be located in the City of New York, for the purpose of establishing and maintaining in said city a Museum and library of art, of encouraging and developing the study of the fine arts, and the application of arts to manufacture and practical life, of advancing the general knowledge of kindred subjects, and, to that end, of furnishing popular instruction."

The Museum at the Fashion Institute of Technology, New York
www.fitnyc.edu
Find inspiration from an eclectic mix of everything to do with fashion. This online resource features some of the most influential, flamboyant and culturally diverse fashion designers.

V&A Museum
www.vam.ac.uk
The V&A Museum, London, is a world-leading museum for design, art, fashion and textiles. It has an impressive online catalogue that brings together historical and contemporary works.

Patterns

Burdastyle
www.burdastyle.com
Find patterns and inspirations from other like-minded individuals. Post questions regarding sewing projects and get involved in the sewing community that Burdastyle offers. Great website for both the inexperienced and experienced.

Colette Patterns
www.Colettepatterns.com
Find great patterns for different abilities, ranging from beginners to intermediate. Styles are retro with a contempopary chic. Subscribe to the blog for instant updates.

Oliver + S
www.oliverands.com
Interactive site, where you can purchase sewing patterns from beginners to the more advanced. Suitable for all ages.

Vogue Patterns
www.voguepatterns.mccall.com
From vintage to contemporary, a range of sewing patterns of differing levels. Features patterns from a range of fashion designers (DKNY, Issey Miyake, Anna Sui). Subscribe to get some of the most up-to-date styles from the catwalks.

Equipment

J&B Sewing Machine Co. Ltd
www.J&Bsewing.com
Domestic and industrial sewing machines, some of which have been reconditioned and are in perfect working order. If ordering, explain what type of machine you want and what will be the main use.

Morplan
www.morplan.com
Sewing equipment such as scissors, thread snips, chalk and so on. Supplies available online or you can request a catalogue for mail order. If you are a student, please mention this so that you can be directed to the student site.

Fabric and trims

Abakhan
www.abakhan.co.uk
Stocks haberdashery, trims and fabrics. They have a section dedicated to dressmaking and tailoring. Items such as trims, braid, sequins, tailor dummies, shoulder pads, boning and corsetry are all available.

Liberty London
www.liberty.co.uk
This iconic store is home to the Liberty fabric, and also houses a gorgeous selection of notions, buttons and trims in its haberdashery department. This beautiful building is worth a visit.

M&J Trimming
1008 Sixth Avenue, New York, NY 10018
www.mjtrim.com
This store has a plethora of notions and trims for any sewing project. You will find contemporary and historical inspired notions. Supplies everything, from buttons to rhinestones.

Purl Soho
459 Broome St, Manhattan, NY 10013, United States
www.purlsoho.com
Chic, contemporary store, great for finding inspiration for any sewing project. Good selection of fabric and trims, as well as dedicated knitting and crafts materials.

MacCulloch & Wallis
www.macculloch-wallis.co.uk
MacCulloch & Wallis is a long-established company, selling fabrics ranging from wool to silks and an abundance of linings, trims and notions.

The Button Queen, London
www.buttonqueen.co.uk
The Button Queen specializes in antique and contemporary buttons.

The Cloth House
www.clothhouse.com
Here you will find fabrics sourced from around the world, as they work very closely with their suppliers. The Cloth House offers a range of fabrics from traditional to contemporary, as well as vintage trims.

Bibliography

Aldhrich, W. 2008.
Metric pattern cutting for
womenswear.
Wiley-Blackwell

Apple. 2005.
Tailoring: A step-by-step
guide to creating beautiful
customized garments.
Apple Press

Bergh, R. 2006.
Make your own patterns: an
easy step-by-step guide to
making over 60 dressmaking
patterns.
New Holland

Ganderton, L. 2011.
The Liberty book of home
sewing.
Chronicle Books

Hirsch, G. 2012.
Gertie's new book for better
sewing: a modern guide to
couture-style sewing using
basic vintage techniques.
Stewart, Tabori and Chang

James, C. 1998.
The complete serger
handbook (new edition).
Sterling

McNicol, A. 2013.
How to use your sewing
machine: an absolute guide
for beginners.
Kyle Craig Publishing

Mitnick, S. 2011.
The Colette sewing
handbook: 5 fundamentals for
a great sewing experience.
Krause Publications

Quinn, M.D.,
Weiss Chase, R. 2002.
Designing without limits:
design and sewing for special
needs (revised 1st edition).
Fairchild Books

Readers Digest. 1997.
The Readers Digest complete
guide to sewing (8th edition).
Readers Digest

Reid, A. 2011.
Stitch magic.
Stewart, Tabori and Chang

Seikatsu Sha, S.T. 2011.
Simple modern sewing:
8 basic patterns to create
25 favourite garments.
Interweave

Turbett, P. 1988.
The techniques of cut
and sew.
Batsford Ltd

Vogue Knitting
Magazine. 2006.
"Vogue" sewing
(revised and updated).
Sixth & Spring Books

Wolf. C., Fanning. R.,
Cooke. R. 1996.
The art of manipulating
fabric.
Krause Publications

Acknowledgements

Thanks:

Nicola Chadwick
Teresa Lovequine-Telfer
Valerie Prendergast
Mark Atkinson
John Lau
Gareth Kershaw
Deanna Clark
Helene Chartrain
Louise Kahrmann
Fern Baldie
Dr Simeon Gill
Victoria Walker
Yvonne Lin
Jonathan Jepson
Alison Lowe (Felicities Ltd)
Ada Zanditon
Hellen Van Rees
Léa Peckre
Nicole Pelletier
Funmilayo Deri
Mada Van Gaans
Louise Bennetts
AFWNY
Hollings Faculty, MMU
Adiat Disu (Adiree.com)
Beate Goodager
Elie Saab
Emma Hardstaff
Kerry Seager (Junky Styling)
Victoria Whittaker
Stefen Ramirez (Inaisce)
Dan WJ Prasad

Special thanks to:
Josephine Brown and
Daniel Prendergast

Picture credits

Laurence Laborie
Front cover

Getty images
3, 8, 10, 11, 17–19, 36, 40, 41, 43,
47–52, 66, 68–70, 72–3, 75, 120,
123, 126–8, 130, 132, 137–8, 144,
147–8, 150–2, 164, 166–71, 174–5

Elie Saab
6, 39, 114–17, 119

Beate Godager
(photographer: Peter Ravnsborg;
design: Beate Godager)
7

Gareth Kershaw
12–13, 38, 122

Nicole Pelletier
(all illustrations copyright
the artist)
15, 16, 20–1, 23–5, 44–6, 56–8,
78–9, 133, 135, 137, 139, 143–6,
149–50, 153

Gütermann Threads
22

Mada Van Gaans
28–9, 31, 33

Louise Bennetts
34, 53, 76–7, 108–13, 131

Fern Baldie
37, 54

Hellen Van Rees
55

Matthieu Melin
(designer: Qui Hao)
59

Jennifer Prendergast
25, 26, 27, 61, 81

Ada Zanditon
62–5

V & A
@ Victoria and Albert
Museum, London
74

Jonathan Jepson
82–5

Dan WJ Prasad
86, 88–9, 125, 134

Yvonne Lin
(photographer: Michelle Kuan;
model: Christine MacGibbon;
MUA: Amanda Blair)
90–1, 93–5, 135

Emma Hardstaff
96–101, 141

Funmilayo Deri
(Funlayo Déri Venturs Ltd.)
102–7, 139–40

Léa Peckre
(photographer: Pascal Montary)
124, 158–63

Kerry Seager
(photographer: Ness Sherry)
129

Victoria Whittaker
154–6

Simeon Gill
(Simeon Gill using TC2 body
scanning software)
172–3